The King of

THE KING OF INSTRUMENTS

How Churches Came To Have Organs

PETER WILLIAMS

First published in Great Britain 1993
Society for Promoting Christian Knowledge
Holy Trinity Church
Marylebone Road
London NW1 4DU

British Library Cataloguing-in-Publication Data
A catalogue record for this book is available from the British Library

ISBN 0–281–04664–6

Typeset by Watermark, Cromer, Norfolk
Printed in Great Britain by
The Cromwell Press, Melksham, Wiltshire

'What?' [Herr Stein said.] 'A man like you, so fine a clavier-player, wants to play on an instrument which has no douceur, no expression, no piano, no forte, but is always the same?' 'That does not matter', I replied. 'In my eyes and ears the organ is the king of instruments.'

Letter of Wolfgang Amadeus Mozart to his father, 17 October 1777

Contents

Foreword

In the course of writing *The Organ in Western Culture, 750–1250* (Cambridge University Press), I began to feel that the essentials of a fascinating story could easily get lost in all the musicological and other detail necessary for such a book. Accordingly, with the encouragement of Judith Longman of SPCK, I have taken salient points from the story and attempted to recount it in a different way, emphasizing certain points in the history and nature of Western Christianity as they relate to the organ and its music.

But I discovered that telling a story in a different way also means telling a somewhat different story. For example, it became necessary to show what is unexpected or unique about organs, mainly by asking questions about how the Church came to have them, what for, why that particular part of the Church, and what difference they made to music. In order to develop these ideas I have put more emphasis on what it was an early saint like St Aldhelm would have known of organs when he described one, and on what were the major influences on monks and clerics. In particular, I have concluded that St Augustine's psalm-commentary must have been a crucial factor in the Western Church's having organs. Although I avoided writing a Conclusion at the end, which would inevitably have been simplistic, conjectures are made throughout the book and, I hope, serve to give some idea of where the answers to the question might lie.

In trying to make the outlines of the story clear, I felt it necessary to keep two specialist elements more or less intact. First, it is important to give both the text of the Latin authors and translations of what they say, because translating is interpreting. These documents are all we have, and yet so often their meaning is so ambiguous that any English version of what they say ought not to be taken as the sole authority. On the other hand, leaving them untranslated would leave too many questions begged. Second, if their implications are to be shown, neither music nor organ-building can be discussed successfully without some of the technical language belonging to each of them. With *A Layman's Guide to Space-Time Theory* one can get only so far without a knowledge of vectors and their technical language; in attempting to understand the significance of the organ keyboard and its construction, one comes to a similar if less forbidding impasse. Nevertheless, I have tried to keep technicalia to a minimum.

In writing this account, I am particularly indebted to Mr J. Samuel Hammond, Rare Book Librarian and Carilloneur of Duke University, North Carolina, for comments and help. I trust he will not take personally my doubts about the musical potential of bells.

Peter Williams
June 1992

Catalonia = inland from Barcelona
Kent = around Canterbury
Normandy = around Rouen
Wessex = around Winchester

Aa	Aachen	Col	Cologne	PA	PANNONIA
Ab	Abingdon	Com	Compiègne	Pa	Paris
Al	St. Albans	FRA	FRANCIA	Ra	Ramsey
Ar	Arras	FRI	FRISIA	Re	Reichersberg
Au	Augsburg	G	Gloucester	Rh	Rheims
Be	S. Benet-de-Bages	GER	GERMANIA	R	Rochester
Bo	Bologna	Gh	Ghent	Ro	Rouen
Br	Bruges	Gl	Glastonbury & Wells	S	Silchester
Bro	Brogne	Go	Gorze	SA	SAXONIA
BU	BURGUNDY	Ha	Hautvillers	SJ	S Juan-las-Abadesas
C	Canossa	He	Helmarshausen	So	Soissons
CA	CANTÁBRICA	Ko	Konstanz,	St-A	St-Amand
Ca	Canterbury		Petershausen & Reichenau	St-D	St-Denis
Cl	Clermont	L	Lobbes	St-E	Bury St. Edmunds
Co	Corvey	La	Laon	St-R	St-Riquier
		M	Malmesbury	Str	Strasbourg
		Mi	Mildenhall/Water Newton	SU	SUAVIANS
		Mo	Montserrat	To	Toul
		Mu	Murbach	Vi	Vich
		Ne	Nennig	W	Winchester and Salisbury
		P	Paderborn	We	Werden

BLACK SEA

CASPIAN SEA

...ANTINE — Constantinople

EMPIRE

ARMENIA

ASIA MINOR

Antioch

SASSANID EMPIRE

...A N I A N

Basra

PERSIAN GULF

Alexandria

Jerusalem

Bethlehem

A R A B S

COPTS

R. Nile

Introduction

Christendom

If in the early seventh century, on the eve of the Muslim advance, a traveller had crossed Christendom from Iona in Scotland to Basra on the Persian Gulf, or from Georgia down through Asia Minor and across the Mediterranean to Spain, or from the lands of the Copts to those of the Angles, he would have seen no organs in churches anywhere. Not in the great churches of Jerusalem or Constantinople, not in the basilicas of Rome or the monasteries of Syria, and of course not in hermitages on the banks of the River Nile or Shannon, would one have heard the sound of organs. The only possible exception – and this only in some major Eastern city such as Jerusalem or Constantinople – would have been if on a special occasion some great and pompous outdoor procession had brought a few instruments with it into the nave or aisles of a church located on the route (a 'station'). These instruments would have been part of the furnishings for a procession, remaining only until it moved out again or disbanded.

Since the emperor or bishop participating in such processions knew that the psalms mentioned *organa*, he would not necessarily think musical instruments in principle unseemly at religious events of the more public and boisterous kind. But people also associated the sound of instruments with other kinds of rowdy event: street-carnivals, hippodromes and theatres. Even if imperial games in the hippodrome had something of a semi-sacred character because of the holiness of the emperor's person, elsewhere instruments meant licentious behaviour of one kind or another, and in much of the former Roman Empire there must have lingered a folk-memory of the particular way in which organs had contributed to the now infamous games. So many uses to which instruments were put were foreign to Christian practice that organs must have been slow to enter churches in any region where they had been familiar before Christianity or were still familiar outside it.

If on the eve of the First Crusade nearly half a millennium later (1095) the same journey had been made – but now including northern Christendom, with central-eastern Europe and the western steppe – there would still have been no church organs anywhere *except* in one particular area: that sector or northwest quarter of a circle radiating from Rome and stretching as far north as the English Wash. Here by then were several well-documented church *organa* and, one can assume, many more that were not documented. How did this come about? Why should they be known only in this area? What did they do, and where did they do it? What were they like? Is the organ known throughout the world today purely because of the global role played in later centuries by this very part of Europe?

It is with such questions as these that this book will attempt to deal. While what happened and when are unlikely ever to be quite certain, several previous misunderstandings can be corrected and some focus given to a curiously complicated, wide-ranging subject.

Organs in Christian Europe

The church organ was so specific to the northwestern sector radiating out from Rome that it is unlikely the Eternal City itself had one as early as the First Crusade. At least, there is no clear record of one. It is quite possible that memories of the hippodrome and how the organ had contributed to its unholy events lingered more vividly there than elsewhere and kept it back from entering churches in Rome itself, or even the big courtyards of its basilicas. Besides, particularly in the decades before and after the Saracens sacked St Peter's in 853, Rome was hardly Western Christendom's centre for technology, even if it did see some of its churches rebuilt and restored in that century. The Crusade itself, declared in a French city by a French Cluniac pope, can be regarded as a Roman movement only by proxy.

Nor did the original centres of Christianity play much of a

part in the history of the church organ either before or after the Persian and Muslim conquests of the seventh century. In Byzantine provinces or in Antioch and Alexandria (cities like Rome claiming to be the seat of the apostle Peter), people may still occasionally have heard street-organs or even high-pressure sirens such as were made by secular craftsmen; and these instruments may have been known by the name *organa* or some Arabic equivalent (meaning 'device', 'apparatus', or 'special equipment'). But they were not church organs and had nothing to do with Christian services, any more than they did with the ceremonies of the synagogue or, later, of the mosque. Not to the Greeks, Jews, early Christians, Byzantines, Persians or Arabs can the eventual development of the organ, including its familiar keyboard and all that this led to, be attributed.

It is not so much a question of why organs were never known in the Orthodox Church or in the parts of Christendom overrun by Muslims, as how they got known in the West. How did they come to be built in Winchester and Rheims and Cologne, far away from the centres of culture and technology in the eastern Mediterranean? If Rome itself had little to do with this technological and musical development, what did? Part of the answer must be that it was their very remove from old centres of culture which led Western Christians to develop various things – objects, practices, customs – that were quite alien to original Christianity, including eventually the making of church organs.

The part of Christendom with the first church organs was the one whose technologies and sciences were so to develop as to lead to the very way 'technology and science' are defined and used in common parlance today. Not the original Mediterranean Christianity, but that flourishing northwest of Rome was the one in which the development of keyboards and musical notations came to appear normal, achievements of Western monasteries usually founded or re-founded as Benedictine. Though claiming authority from a southern hermit (St Benedict, †c.550) and a Roman pope (St Gregory †604), the Order was particularly effective farther north, in the lands of the Franks, the Angles, the Saxons and the Suavians. By 1000 the monasteries had produced the biggest single set of musical innovations known in history: a whole repertory of chant, a new practical theory of music, a fixing once and for all of the musical scale as we know it in the West, new musical styles such as sequences, new genres such as liturgical drama, and – ultimately the most important of all – a more flexible way of notating music than any previously known.

This is a story in which the organ played a part, not necessarily to perform in any of the music but as another manifestation of the monasteries' self-taught inventiveness, of the ability of their monks to embrace all in the religious life, and of their doing so mostly in a primitive area far from the sun and light of the Mediterranean.[1] Like other imaginative achievements of this culture, organs came to play a part in the West's assumption that time equals development – that one must constantly apply and stretch technology, whether of musical instruments, movable type, steam engines, particle accelerators, or anything else.

The three particular technologies needed for making an organ – to produce air-under-pressure, to transfer the hand's motion to other planes, and to make medium-hard metal pipes – would each be open to constant 'improvement'. The work of monastic and other craftsmen would not stand still, and their techniques would not be secreted away or regarded as the exclusive property of rulers, like Chinese porcelain-crafts under the mandarins. Technique would not be fixed or guarded by myth or mystery, and any large monastery would be able to specialize in a range of skills, including those relevant to making organs. No bishop or abbot had a monopoly of such skills, and by c.1000 there are likely to have been several centres of interest in organs, quite probably independent of each other in their design-techniques and producing various lines of development of their own.

In such respects as these the organ becomes a paradigm of early Western technological development. In considering the period around 1000, it is hardly an exaggeration to say that although Western technology was then beginning to

[1] One could make comparable points about church-building. While in 525 the West worshipped in hovels compared to the church of Hagia Sophia then being constructed in Constantinople, six hundred years or so later the Benedictine builders of the Abbey of St-Denis were achieving the miracle of high gothic vaults, known only in the West.

develop over a broad front, usually by means of inventions originally made elsewhere, nevertheless a large organ with bellows, keys and pipes was among the most complicated and difficult pieces of equipment made anywhere in the world at the time. A great monastic church with an organ in it for the people to see and hear was wittingly or unwittingly saluting the Maker of All Things with the world's most advanced apparatus. In some cases this must have been its prime function, for monastic churches were public exhibition spaces as nothing else at the time was, particularly in the climate of northwest Europe. They alone could bring wonders mechanical or spiritual to the attention of the people, and in this respect organs had something in common with the relics of saints ceremoniously deposited in the same great churches and performing miracles for pilgrims visiting them. Mechanical wonders cannot have seemed entirely distinct from spiritual, for sound itself is intangible, numinous and mysterious, linking the listener with the life immaterial.

Each of the three organ-technologies of wind, mechanism and pipes had been mastered (at least on a small scale) by the Hellenic engineers of Alexandria, and perhaps also by the ancient Greeks, although this is less certain than it once appeared to be. The great sirens described in later Arabic sources (see chapter 2) were the product of specialized craftsmen in the same basic technologies. If any such siren-instruments ever got built for use on the battlefield, as one assumes they did, many in the opposing armies must have been terrified. But terror can take the form of Holy Terror, and an element in the Christian adoption of organs must have been the awesome nature of all mechanically produced sound, a sound louder than anything directly produced by the ordinary breath of men. To this day, a grand concluding organ voluntary in a reverberant church can still convey that awe.

Besides, not only was a Western organ not technologically inferior to, say, a great Burmese or Korean bell cast at immense trouble or cost and hung by means of the most ingeniously arranged levers and pulleys, it also had an infinitely greater musical potential. It would help to form the nature of all subsequent music as no bell or siren could ever have done.

Historical 'Evidence'

Much of this interpretation of organ-history is conjectural because for nearly twenty centuries, from ancient Greece to Renaissance Europe, there is an unbridgeable gap between what is documented about the instrument and what must have actually happened. It has been usual for written histories to make this unbridgeable gap appear as small as they could. But one might more usefully give it due emphasis and ask why some things get written down and some do not.

To assume that the complicated hydraulic organs of the Greeks were known before simpler instruments just because the written record describes the former and never the latter is in effect to deny that there is a gap between what is documented and what must have been known. This leads inevitably to a misunderstanding of what happened. Many basic crafts such as carpentry never get described in connection with anything, and to this day the origin of one of the most conspicuous parts in the familiar church organ – its wooden casework – is totally unknown and cannot be documented, despite what one hopes are educated guesses about the history of church furnishings. By looking at samples of the various kinds of evidence in the centuries either side of 1000, two particular problems with what is called 'evidence' can be recognized.

First, not very much was ever written about organs. Considering the vast number of great churches constructed in that quarter-circle north-west of Rome, there are astonishingly few references of any kind to instruments. This is particularly so before the later thirteenth century, when churches became used to setting up systematic records such as fabric rolls or writing contracts for outside craftsmen. Nevertheless, sparse information absolutely does not prove that organs were otherwise unknown, even if much has to be guessed about where they might have been heard. It must be reasonable to suppose that if a small fenland monastery in tenth-century Anglo-Saxon England (such as Ramsey) had an organ, as documents say it did, then a great abbey of enormous wealth and influence in the centre of our quarter-circle (such as Cluny or St-Denis) did also, even if nothing is known about it. If, on the other hand, it is possible that for centuries the grandest abbeys had no organ because for some reason they were too grand to have any use for such equipment, then that still leaves a vast number of less grand foundations only too pleased, one imagines, to have bells or organs to arouse local curiosity and give a sense of presence.

Whatever the most convincing of these guesses, one of several things would follow from them. If many great abbeys did have an organ that was nowhere documented, then it must have been viewed as ordinary equipment like sundials and bell-clusters.[2] These too were rarely documented but were by no means uncommon: they were equipment usefully contributing in various ways to the liturgy but not actually part of it, rather like organs in this respect. Alternatively, if abbeys had no organ when they could easily have done so, perhaps it was because at first the instrument was viewed as an unimportant crowd-pleaser, unnecessary where the liturgy was pre-eminent and well maintained. In that case, however, the organ could have become as familiar as it was by 1300 only through a sudden spontaneous outburst in many areas at once, with little or no pre-history. On the whole, the first of these guesses seems the more likely: organs were there but documentation about them was not.

The second problem with 'evidence' is that what was written is easily misleading. The many ways in which the word *organum* was used mean that reliable references to organs are even rarer than they may seem at first. What appears to be good documentation can turn out to be useless for present purposes. When sources show a ninth-century pope writing to a German bishop to ask for an *organum*, or an eleventh-century English cathedral chapter having its *organa* suspended for defying the Metropolitan, or something called an *organum* being heard in the services of a thirteenth-century French cathedral, they provide no evidence whatever about organs because the word means something else in each of these documents. (Quite what, is examined in chapter 3.)

Yet the prospect for understanding church practice at the time is not entirely bleak. The very fact that *organum* means

---

[2] 'Clusters', i.e. the groups of large bells for the public, as distinct from the private monastic signal-bell often specified in monastic rules and service ordinals.

many different things, including 'a kind of vocal music' in particular and 'instruments of music' in general, suggests that organs may sometimes have been present or may have contributed to music without anyone taking the trouble to say so. (In this book, 'organum' (not italicized) denotes the early form of counterpoint so called by music historians, while *organum* or *organa* (italicized, and quoted from Latin documents) has the other meanings: instrument, instruments, organs of learning, of authority, the liturgy, the body, etc.) Organs could have 'slipped into' church life as a matter of course if the monastery or cathedral were well enough appointed to have workshops for metal and wood, as so many of them were. There would be no record of payments to craftsmen or to bellows-blowers: if either of these were monks, they were not paid; and if they were secular workmen, it was too early for accounts to have been kept. Whatever the case, there would be no need for permission from the pope or for a ruling from a Council of churches in order for such an instrument to 'slip into' the church and take part in what went on there.

Not only do such *written sources* have to be treated with caution: what it is that *early drawings* of organs are meant to be representing is a complex question, and there is little use taking them as evidence for such-and-such a detail without examining their intentions. In the first place, here too there are astonishingly few examples, and what there are belong to a few genres only. In the second, no manuscript need have been aiming to show anything modern or real or actual. This could also be true for the later medieval period, when miniature drawings become more 'realistic', eagerly portraying various kinds of equipment and working apparatus (organs, watermills, clocks, windmills, carts, ploughs), none of which can be taken merely at face-value.

One such piece of equipment gives an example of the questions arising: the wheelbarrow. Whatever else it was doing, the earliest-known drawing of a wheelbarrow in a psalter (fourteenth century) was certainly signalling a new interest in drawing such gadgetry. Why had no one thought to draw a wheelbarrow before? Either because it did not exist or – likelier – because only from the mid-thirteenth century onwards did it become conventional to make references in illuminated manuscripts to ingenious apparatus of such a kind. By now an artist could draw building equipment like wheelbarrows not (only) because he was interested in them, but in so far as they had become an emblem: they stood for the productivity of a working religious Order in general, or for his own work in particular. Another possibility is that he was striving to be original, not copying a manuscript centuries old but seeking novelty and ingenuity, deliberately arousing curiosity in the psalter's user. Perhaps now it was conscious policy to leave behind the remoter tone of earlier books: his psalter may have had a new kind of use, particularly if he were a friar. In any case, it is quite likely that he would wish to bring all mundane or ingenious devices into a sacred setting, making his own salute as 'a toiler in the vineyard' to the Maker of All Things. Perhaps this particular wheelbarrow artist was one of his monastery's carpenters too.

Whichever of these is the likeliest in this instance, for many a piece of technical equipment the illumination-artists must frequently have worked from written description only.[3] How would one know whether this was the case with the wheelbarrow here? – its period could well have seen the circulation of a treatise on the mechanical arts in which levers and wheels were united in various contrivances used in building-work of various kinds. Furthermore, an artist could make use of both what he had read and what he had seen, and when he did, it would be difficult to disentangle the information and estimate what in it was totally 'real'. All such questions should be borne in mind every time any medieval picture of an organ or other apparatus is scrutinized for the technical information it appears to give.

After the written and pictorial evidence, the *musical*. It used to be assumed that since in some medieval sources a certain kind of vocal music based on the chant was called *organum*, and was directed by an *organista* or a master of the *organizandi*, then it must have had something directly to do

---

[3] That it is still tempting for historians of technology to use medieval illuminations as if they were illustrations of the more modern kind is suggested by e.g. Matthier, where the oldest picture of a wheelbarrow (Chartres, glass of *c.*1220) and the oldest written reference to it (building accounts of Henry III of England, 1222) are mined for technical information without questions being asked about the nature and purpose of documentation at that period.

with the organ. But this is not likely to be true, for reasons discussed further in this book. Nor is it likely that organs were brought into church in order to accompany singing, whether the celebrant's special mass, the lay people's responses, or the brothers' daily and private chant. All that one can be certain about is that they were there to provide sound, but what kind of sound, for what purpose and at what points they provided it can only be conjectured.

The Wider Significance of Organs

It could be that one reason why Western music differs from other musics in various fundamentals, particularly in its 'bass line' serving as the 'root' for 'harmony', is that it alone developed the organ and in particular the organ-keyboard.[4] Since the reasoning behind such an interpretation of history – how music was practised, written down and developed as a consequence of the keyboard – is speculative, I would like to summarize it before returning to the survey of more concrete evidence.

The argument can be framed as follows. Beethoven's Choral Symphony in D minor is conceivable only where there is, among other things, the idea of D minor; this D minor conforms to the Western definition of keys (major/minor tonality), which is dependent on the true perfect cadence, dominant to tonic; and this cadence exists only when there is a bass line. Now a bass line is more than the notes produced by whatever happens to be the lowest voice, for unlike the other voices, it gives 'harmonic support' to the chords above. (It would not be able to do this if it were merely duplicating in the lower octave what a higher voice was singing.) Such a bass line will result quite naturally from a keyboard of several octaves, that is to say a compass longer than that of any other instrument and played by the two hands of a single player. For while a simple chant-melody can be played by either hand, a 'bass' will evolve only for the left as a 'treble' will only for the right.

---

[4] Although all other keyboard instruments are later by far than the organ, the relation between them in the years of expansion around 1400 is not yet clear. It was probably the dimensions and touch of the small portable organ's keyboard that the other instruments (including the larger church organ) all eventually copied.

In addition, the making of deeper (longer) pipes and the creating of music that makes use of them will change the nature of music in general. From being predominantly high and bass-less in sound, as is the case with a good deal of non-Western music to this day, the kind of music produced by such instruments will gradually move towards a wider sound-spectrum, and other 'bass instruments' will appear. Even if organ-compass was slow to go much below tenor c, as was surely the case, performers would be bound to be affected by the bass-and-treble character of a keyboard of several octaves. So therefore would composers. Furthermore, actual pitch-level may be misleading, for an organ-pipe will have a bigger fundamental in the tone than a medieval (or Chinese or Arabic) string instrument, and it will therefore give a better feeling of 'bass'.

It is difficult to demonstrate that had the keyboard not come to have several octaves a bass line could not have evolved. A more compelling argument might be that the written counterpoint emerging in thirteenth- and four-teenth-century Europe naturally created a bass line because its voices were moving in such a way as to produce 'cadences' (restful ends of phrases or sections) with certain characteristics (those recognized later as belonging to the perfect cadence). In such an interpretation of what happened, whichever were the lower notes of the two interweaving voice-parts producing these cadences would eventually be replaced by one consistently low voice. It would be a kind of Lowest Common Multiple bass line, evolving naturally in vocal music and thus independently of keyboards.

And yet, unless there was already some familiarity with the 'bass line' effect, it is not obvious why the lowest notes happening to be produced by crossed voices should become a new kind of single voice. One can imagine how upper voices (treble) might become more and more ornate, how chant – i.e. a melody in the baritone voice – might gradually have more and more complex music superimposed on it. For there were trained alto and treble singers and various treble instruments always ready to embellish in the upper range, as no doubt there had been in Roman times. But why should the bass line, a new concept, develop? For the theory of the Lowest Common Multiple to be plausible one would need to explain why something complex (crossed voices in formal written counterpoint) becomes something simple (a single bass line in all kinds of music) rather than vice versa.

Since written music was (and is) only an individual and formal creation for particular requirements, other musics could long have been simpler in this respect, moving towards the idea of bass line as the keyboard became familiar or as the technology came for producing 'bass notes' from long pipes or strings. On any keyboard there is a natural tendency towards held or slow-moving notes at the bottom because increased length means slower speech, and this would have been more noticeable when much deeper sounds became normal in the organs of many larger churches from about 1400 onwards. Any 'harmonically orientated bass' heard in the written counterpoint of an Obrecht (†1505) would surely not have been new to organists several generations earlier as they learned to exploit the big bass pipes at Halberstadt or Rouen. These and others like them were the deepest man-made sounds that had ever been heard, deeper than those of any other regular instrument (including those of folk-music), and giving a sound that had no agility for treble melody. Even with a more modest compass of three octaves or so the lower pipes would also produce a bass to 'support' the harmony.

While anyone can sing a fourth or fifth, frequent leaps of this kind are far less characteristic of the ends of most types of chant than they are of later instrumental bass lines. Rather than the perfect cadence *being abstracted* from the beautifully shaped lines of formal counterpoint, it seems easier to suppose that composers of counterpoint shaped their lines and crossed voices in order to produce the kind of bass line *already familiar* at cadences when, for example, the organist improvised at festive masses. And not only improvised: in transcribing vocal music – probably his most formal music – the organist would produce from whatever was the lowest voice at each moment a line that would acclimatize the ear to the idea of 'harmonic root' long before the music of Obrecht and his generation.

There is a further consideration. Since a row of keys does not have to be in one sequence from low to high,[5] or be made up of repeated octaves, the Western organ as it evolved represented only one particular idea of what a keyboard might be. But it was one on which both a *bass line* and a *soprano melody* could be played, and one that would more and more distinguish between the two. Obviously the keyboard made up of octave blocks of sound was one that would once and for all confirm the idea of the musical scale as a sequence of octaves,[6] and it seems unlikely that the organ-builders of antiquity had always constructed in this way. Once the sound-spectrum was seen by music's practitioners (organ-makers and players) as a sequence of octaves, irrespective of what a theorist might teach, the scene was set for the development of Western music.

Conclusion

Whatever one might speculate about its origins, the bass line remains one of the most extraordinary of all Western inventions, unforeseen by the Benedictine reformers of the tenth century when they put organs in their churches. But the organ became a large instrument – and thus acquired such musical significance – only because part of the Christian Church brought it within its doors, whereupon it could grow and develop beyond the wildest imagination of the ancient Greek engineers. It is otherwise difficult to see why or how the compass of the organ would have become more than an octave, or at most two octaves. Only when it no longer needed to be portable would Western craftsmen learn to make large pipes for it, doing so as a matter of course and habit in one abbey or cathedral church after another. Only when organs got into church could they regularly contribute to its service music and widen the whole scope of what it was that music could do.

In such matters as these the question How did churches come to have organs? becomes central to many others.

[5] It is possible that the late tenth-century keyboard at Winchester was not so: see below, p.119.
[6] This would be the case particularly since the set of pipes for each note of an organ (its 'chorus') was made up of accumulated unisons and octaves, eventually with some pipes sounding the twelfth as well in order to fill in a certain bareness of sound given by octaves alone.

Perhaps its biggest contribution is to suggest that the history of music is not (only) the history of an art or even strictly of a science, but (also) the history of technology, and of quite specific technologies. For example, if the Choral Symphony of Beethoven can be related to keyboards in the way suggested, it means that it is a direct beneficiary of the thirteenth-century organ-builder's grasp of pewter technology, for it was this and only this that enabled him to make larger pipes than he ever could with copper, and thus to give deeper sounds than anyone before had ever regularly heard.

2

Organs Before They Became Church Instruments

Since for present purposes what antique organs of various kinds bequeathed to Christendom is as important as how they were constructed, certain sections in this chapter will summarize the purposes they may have served in Rome, Byzantium and elsewhere. However, technical questions about the more complicated antique organs – hydraulic- or water-organs – also require summary, if only because the eventual Christian organ seems to have been independent of them, drawing on less elevated, perhaps illiterate traditions. Some of the technical discussion that follows is directed particularly at readers familiar with how organs work.

The Roman Water-Organ

There are three main kinds of evidence for Greek and Roman organs as known before the collapse of imperial Rome: pictorial (mosaics, carvings, terracotta pieces, coins), literary (poems, miscellanies, inscriptions, biographies, psalm-commentaries) and technical (treatises on the mechanical arts or *artes mechanicae*). Seldom is it clear what the previous source of information was for any piece of evidence in any of these three categories, and one can certainly not assume that any artist or author knew an actual object of the kind he was dealing with. All these forms of information could well be describing not actual organs but 'constructs' created by artists or authors and made familiar by them, while all the time makers themselves were successfully producing various other types of instrument, and doing so well into the later periods of the Byzantine and even Turkish empires. By chance, a little organ of third-century Pannonia (Hungary) has survived to suggest instrument-making of a kind for which there is no clear evidence in any of the three main types of evidence listed above (see pp. 112–14).

Technical details in the mechanical treatises repay attention, not least since one of them, the *De architectura* of Vitruvius, circulated in the ninth-century monasteries of the ex-Roman Empire in the West. This is the treatise above all others that helped inspire the Western idea of *technical description*, which in turn led eventually to the instruction manual and the blueprint of a later age. Also important, however, is that since none of the *ars mechanica* treatises gives anything like a full description of how to make an organ, practical Christian craftsmen of the tenth century must have created instruments irrespective of what their literate colleagues in monastery libraries happened to be reading about and re-copying.

Vitruvius's *De architectura* is thought to have been written or compiled in the middle of the first century BC, becoming known in England by the late eighth century, and circulating far and wide by the twelfth. It includes advice on matters of practical acoustics (Book 1), on the Greek theory concerning the notes of music (Book 5), and on various mechanical devices using air and water power (Book 10). This last book has a section entitled *De hydraulicis* in which a water-organ is described, an apparatus with two major parts. These parts are described only in words, and, like other ancient authors, Vitruvius seems to have left his readers to visualize for themselves how things might be arranged. This method of presentation had the great benefit – unknown since the Renaissance and especially the world of modern patents – of leaving both big and small detail to the ingenuity or the usual practices of the craftsman.

First, a sealed bronze cistern is fitted with an interior vessel which can be filled with pressurized air (wind) driven into it by a pair of pistons-and-cylinders. This interior vessel, open at the bottom, sits in the water which partly fills the cistern; this water rises and falls as the volume of air in the vessel changes, and thus keeps the pressure of the air constant, stabilizing it. Second, this wind passes up into an organ-chest in the top of which are four, six or eight channels, running the length of it, each with its own valve and each with a row of pipes above. Perforated and well-oiled metal sliders (*regulae*) run laterally over these channels, moving under the pipes belonging to each note, admitting wind when their holes tally with the pipes above and blocking it when they do not. They are pulled out and pushed back by hand; or a spring (*pinna*) pushes them back; or they are pulled-and-pushed by little levers ('keys') attached to them in some way, a row of keys now pressed by fingers and made to return by a spring (a 'keyboard').

While any such summary as this disguises many ambiguities in the text, one detail stands out: the only thing Vitruvius says about pipes (which he calls *organa*) is that they are inserted into metal rings soldered on to the bronze chest. (This could have been to keep them in place on an instrument that was moved about a great deal.) Perhaps pipes were the concern of a different craftsman or, more likely, were made according to craftsmen's traditions such as needed no describing in a treatise composed for literate architects.

The most evocative and contentious detail in the *De architectura* concerns the longitudinal channels: for if Vitruvius is saying what later scholars have assumed, he is speaking of four or six or eight rows of pipes *each of which* can be separately played, for the sake of the 'many varieties of melody' created 'by the musical arts' (*e musicis artibus multiplicibus modulorum*). If this is so, then Western European organs took a backward step until their makers reinvented separate stops sixteen hundred years later. But it may not be so, for the details are puzzling. What use was such variable sound in a noisy outdoor theatre organ of the kind Vitruvius seems to be describing? Why four, six or eight rows of pipes but not three, five or seven? If they were not all separate, but could be played at three volume-levels (four, six and eight rows), the same question could be asked. A bigger question is: Even if they were all separate, how do we know they were meant to play together – did they have the same pitch and were they tuned to the same scale?

It is true that four to eight pipes per note would not be incompatible with some extant terracotta models of Roman organs,[1] but for all anyone knows, such models were based not on actual organs but on readings of the *De architectura* or

---

[1] These models were oil lamps, illustrated in Perrot 1971: plates XII and XIII.

some similar material. Perhaps the best guess is that the author/compiler was confused by his source of information, which either was in Greek or its technical terms were. Perhaps he was merely meaning to say that the notes were those of a diatonic or 'white note scale', and that organs used the four notes of the tetrachord (e.g. DEFG), the six notes of the hexachord (as it was also called in later music theory – CDEFGA) and/or the eight of the octave (CDEFGABc), as in the following example:

Example 1

Vitruvius himself implies that written accounts are limited, when he says at the end of his account of the water-organ:[2]

Quodsi qui parum intellexerit ex scriptis,	Anyone who has understood too little from what is written [here],
cum ipsam rem cognoscet,	will find, when he is acquainted
profecto inveniet	with the thing itself, that
curiose et subtiliter	it is curiously and ingeniously
omnia ordinata.	contrived in all respects.

In other words, if you want to know what a water-organ is and how it works, look at one. It is likely that when Vitruvius's treatise became known to the builders of Charlemagne's chapel at Aachen in *c*.800, as it did, they paid attention only to the treatise's sections dealing with architecture and pro-portional design, taking no steps to build a hydraulic organ according to its instructions. There is nothing unusual in this: no source of pictorial, literary or technical information about Roman and Greek organs can ever be shown to have led to instruments of exactly the same sort being built expressly for churches in either the Christian West or the Christian East.

[2] Vitruvius text in Callebat; for translation, see also Morgan.

The Greek Water-Organ

The standard Greek account of the water-organ is found in Chapter 42 of Book 1 of a treatise on pneumatic devices, the *Pneumatika* of Hero of Alexandria (see Schmidt), and has been dated to a century or so after Vitruvius. Both could have come directly or indirectly from a Greek treatise attributed to the 'organ's inventor' Ctesibius in the fourth century BC, and both might have circulated in different forms in Mediterranean centres before being 'fixed' in their present form by Western scribes. As a voluminous Greek treatise on a narrow topic, Hero's description does not compare with Vitruvius's for influence in the medieval West, but parts of it were known to Arab translators, and indirectly to at least one tenth-century compiler in a Western monastery (see p.104).

Hero describes only one cylinder, but since he fails to mention the outlet valve preventing the wind from being sucked back on the next stroke, he seems not to be describing every element that one might expect. So directions for cylinders would apply for two as for one. One thirteenth-century copy has a drawing showing eight pipes on the chest, the drawing in a still later manuscript only seven, but since both numbers have musical significance, such diagrams may represent only Western medieval conjecture about what was a correct sequence of notes for an organ:

seven notes: C D E F G A B-flat
eight notes: C D E F G A B-flat B-natural

(see also Musical Example 1, opposite). Hero refers to pipes as *auloi*, which might or might not mean reeds. The most interesting mechanical detail described – only in principle and by no means in full working detail – is the spring-loaded key. What is pressed down by the fingers is the top surface of a pivoted *square* (an L-shaped piece of wood) made to return to position by a spring. The lower end of this rocking square pushes and pulls a 'keyboard' slider, the perforated metal strip also known to Vitruvius.

Here then is the classic invention of the *keyboard with returning keys*, and a major question is: Since Hero (or someone dependent on him) is the only source to mention it before Western European contracts of the fourteenth century, was

19

it otherwise unknown? This seems out of the question, for silence in the documentation cannot be proof that something did not exist. Neither Vitruvius nor the later Benedictine author Theophilus concerns himself with woodwork on this small scale, for it was something that could easily be devised by a carpenter or joiner. The major concern for organ-makers would be the sliders themselves, as they were for the Winchester poet in c.1000 commenting on how the organ was played: he too seems to be describing the movement of the sliders, and one cannot tell whether they had press-keys operating them. (For Theophilus and Winchester, see chapter 5.) Only the little Roman terracotta models hint at keyboards, but it is not possible to tell whether they had spring-loaded keys. Perhaps the artists themselves did not know.

The question of the keys raises a more basic question about early documentation: If pictures and descriptions of the Roman and Greek organ are concerned almost exclusively with the water-organ, does that mean that only it existed? Since bellows were familiar in other connections and were easier to make, it seems more than likely that both small and large bellows-organs were also known – perhaps, for the same reasons, better or more widely known. When St Augustine mentions bellows-organs, or when the carvings on the obelisk of Theodosius show them (see below), it can hardly mean that they were new to the fourth century AD and unknown to the earlier Romans of East or West.

This is a question that bears on the later organ of the Western Church, for if it had bellows rather than a water-cistern – except when someone like Gerbert of Rheims experimented with hydraulics, as well he might (see chapter 3) – it was apparatus that could have been improvised here and there according to crafts surviving across the ex-Roman Empire. Craftsmen were familiar enough with working the basic materials of wood and leather. For a bellows-organ they did not require the kind of skilled metallurgy necessary for casting cisterns and grinding pistons, only normal processes for making the thin-walled pipes and the iron mandrels on which smaller pipes were fashioned. (For pipes longer than three or four feet, hardwood mandrels were easier to make and lighter to use.) It is not difficult to imagine that Attic,

Hellenistic, Roman and Arabic craftsmen had more methods of making organs work than ever got described in treatises, that little bellows-organs had been made all along. Organs do not have to be hydraulic, and it is unlikely that more than a minority of them ever were.

Finally, various glimpses of how organs were used in the civilized cities of the Mediterranean are given by various late classical sources. Where there were Christians, they too would have heard organs played and would conceivably have made use of them for those (few) events from which their pious exclusiveness did not keep them away. Thus the night-time serenades out of doors in January, in which organs could be heard louder than other instruments according to a fifth-century poem from Antioch (Farmer: 48–50), sound like an ancestor of the pre-Lenten carnival. At royal banquets in late Roman times organs were apparently so common that in 454 the bishop of Clermont, Sidonius Apollinaris, could actually praise the Arian Christian king Theodoric II for not making use of them on such occasions (MGH AA 8.31). Clearly, a pagan or heretic Christian would have been expected to use such rowdy little instruments. Weddings were well known for their *organa* (references in Perrot 1965: 95f) and for the licentious festivity which instruments were there to encourage, hence perhaps the fifth-century tales of St Cecilia and St Agnes summarized in chapter 3.

Other occasions for *organa* include processions or ceremonial arrivals of Roman emperors or consuls, various kinds of arena-sports as pictured in the Nennig and Zliten mosaics, and popular acclamations for the ruler (Schuberth: 45f). The *organa* documented for various kinds of outdoor events would certainly have included organs from time to time, perhaps even generally. Particularly interesting are the imperial acclamations, for when the Emperor Caracalla was saluted with sound on his arrival in Alexandria in 215 (Schuberth: 18), he was following a practice that became a model for Frankish kings, bishops and abbots several centuries later.

Whatever their sounds were actually like – orderly shouts, screeching instruments, rhythmically beaten chords, sustained sirens? – processions and the music that accompanied them were a normal manifestation of the community and its life. Little high-pressure hydraulic organs must have been invaluable.

Some Psalm-Commentators

For Western European religious writers and artists, what the psalm-commentaries of St Augustine, St Jerome and Cassiodorus told them about ceremony and customs was paramount. Their influence with respect to organs was crucial for a reason now difficult to grasp: for northerners, they were transmitting the exotic. In recounting various details of various Mediterranean practices to later northern Christianity, they were giving to most readers information that may have impinged little on daily life in the monasteries but would have aroused a degree of interest, not least in organs. What they say is in its way technical and practical, and from time to time craftsmen would have been inspired by their words.

For Psalm 150, Augustine (†430) speaks of *organum* in the sense of instruments in general, and then adds:

quamvis	although
jam obtinuerit consuetudo	now the custom would hold
ut organa proprie dicantur	for calling 'organs' specifically
ea quae inflantur follibus.	those that are winded by bellows.
(PL 37.1964)	

This is a simple but crucial statement. It was not the bellows but the hydraulic organ of which classical Latin authors had spoken, and the greatest of the Latin *artes mechanicae* books had even described its principles of construction, up to a point. But these few words of Augustine offered in effect a Christian interpretation of what it was that the psalms appeared to make legitimate, i.e. the special participation of instruments, furthermore of a kind not known from *artes mechanicae* traditions. This must have been of interest to those musical readers in northwest Europe who can have had no idea that Jewish and early Christian liturgies themselves did not use organs regularly, if at all.

After Augustine, bellows become a part of the definition of organs. They had one advantage as far as his readers were concerned: familiar in other connections, bellows were not so remote or puzzling as the hydraulic cisterns of the textbooks. It is no accident that centuries later even the most derivative and unreal drawings of organs in the Middle Ages generally give their most 'reliable' details for the bellows themselves. Pipes and keyboards can be hopelessly unreal in a drawing, while bellows realistically evoke the hearth or the forge. In addition, Augustine's simple remarks do rather confirm that water-organs, though useful as emblems of imperial or more local power, were not as common as bellows-organs, which needed no technical literature.

The few words devoted to organs in the commentary on Psalm 136/137 by St Jerome (†420) were equally basic to the northwest European reader's knowledge. Using the organ as a time-honoured allegory – the physical body of man is itself an instrument or *organum* – Jerome suggests that the 'musical order' it produces is a form of offering. Just as the instrument

modulatione	through musical order
melos mittit,	produces melody [?],
ita et organum nostrum habemus	so we have our organ
tactum: per ipsum,	to hand: through it [the body],
hoc est per opera,	that is through its works,
melos et canticum	we bring melody, a canticle [?],
et hymnum referimus Deo.	a hymn to God.
(PL 26.1304)	

Although the point of these words is to say that actual organs are not necessary, that it is through our acts themselves *(opera)*[3] that we offer a 'well-regulated hymn' *(modulatione, hymnum)*, one can nevertheless learn something about them. Whatever their pagan associations and however they were reputed to be loud screeching noise-producers, organs could produce *melos* through their keys. Their keyboard enabled the sound to be made orderly and melodic, and presumably was meant to do so. In addition, allegory itself would help the instrument to become acceptable, for if it produced such *well-modulated* sounds in church, it would express man's *works for God* and be desirable for that reason alone.

A third brief but influential reference in psalm-commentaries

---

[3] Perhaps there was some word-link in Jerome's thoughts here: *opera* (works) = *ergon* (work) = *organon* = *organum?*

is the most technical: after Augustine and Jerome had implied that organs were or could become acceptable, Cassiodorus (†c.585) in writing on Psalm 150 must have increased the curiosity of those whose interest was already aroused. Bellows and pipes create a plentiful sound, he says,

et ut eam modulatio	and for this sound to be
decora componat,	properly regulated,
linguis quibusdam	the organ is constructed with
ligneis ab interiore parte	certain wooden tongues in its
construitur, quas	interior, which
disciplinabiliter magistrorum	being controlled methodically
digiti reprimentes,	by masters' fingers,
grandisonam efficiunt et	produce a loud-sounding and
suavissimam cantilenam.	very agreeable melody.
(PL 70.1052–3)	

It is particularly useful to find *suavis* here in conjunction with *grandisonam*, for it implies that organ-sound can be properly ordered (i.e. with a regular keyboard) and its sound both forceful and sweet (i.e. well-toned and well-tuned). Clearly, a reader in *c.*1000 would understand from all this that the organ could produce a chant-melody if required and that it could do so with a penetrating sound – for an outside procession, for a service in the church quire or for the teaching of singers, as the case might be.

The reference to wooden sliders or wooden keys operating sliders is meant to explain how individual notes can be made to sound by the organist, and it could be that the phrase *magistrorum digiti* means that the notes were played by individual fingers. To comment at all at this time on the inner workings of any piece of technical apparatus is most unusual, but Cassiodorus is not the last monk who had an interest in how instruments work. In the same commentary he even remarks on what organs look like, as if he were familiar with at least one example:

organum itaque est quasi	thus the organ is like a kind of
turris.	[castle?] tower.

This implies a tall wooden structure, evidently something developed rather beyond the kind of altar-shape for organs mentioned by Vitruvius. Whatever exactly it was that

Cassiodorus meant by *turris*, it is not unlikely that the artist of the Stuttgart Psalter in *c.*830 had this description in mind when he drew a pair of organs for the final two psalms (see chapter 5): they are tall, have a crowded row of pipes from tall to short (*diversis fistulis*, in Cassiodorus's words), are fed by some prominent bellows and show various wooden parts at hand-level.

Although one could not take the words of any early psalm-commentator as evidence that the organ was used in churches of the fifth or sixth century, there is an important point to bear in mind: they did not forbid it for their later readers. On the contrary, there might lie here an explanation of how the organ did become a church instrument: tenth-century cantors of northwestern Benedictine Europe had organs built in order to take up what it was they interpreted the early, authoritative Mediterranean psalm-commentators as describing and therefore in effect recommending to later Christians.

A Christian Poet

On the basis of what they knew of Mediterranean instruments, or had read about them in early Christian authors such as Tertullian (†*c.*225), various later writers of northern European Christianity refer to the organ in a variety of ways. It is seldom clear whether they knew actual instruments, had merely read about them or had seen representations – perhaps sometimes all three, like a writer of today, but this was surely rare. But in any case, it is never clear how far each kind of source is independent of the others. What follows is a look at one particular poet's reference to organs and at the kind of questions that can be asked about it and many another.

The early saint of Malmesbury, St Aldhelm (†709), wrote the following in his poem *Carmen de virginitate* (Song of Virginity, in MGH AA 15.2.355–6):

> *si vero quisquam chordarum respuit odas,*
> But if anyone disdains the music of strings,
> *et potiora cupit, quam pulset pectine chordas,*
> and prefers something better than the plucking of strings by a plectrum

quis Psalmista pius psallebat cantibus olim,
with which the pious psalmist [David] once accompanied himself,
ac mentem magno gestit modulamine pasci,
and eagerly desires to feed his mind with a great harmoniousness [?],
et cantu gracili refugit contentus adesse,
refusing to be content with a meagre melody [?],
maxima millenis auscultans organa flabris,
let him listen to the greatest *organa* with a thousand breaths,
mulceat auditum ventosis follibus iste,
let it delight his hearing with bellows full of wind,
quamlibet auratis fulgescant caetera capsis.
as in other ways it gleams with its gilt chests.[4]

This sounds at first as if he is recommending organs to accompany psalm-singing in church, but a rereading soon leaves this very doubtful. A bigger question is: Had Aldhelm ever seen an organ – the instrument with bellows – inside or out of church? While his words have often been taken to mean that the English knew the church organ at a period when few others did, much more likely is that Aldhelm was merely alluding to one of the well-known psalm-commentaries. This would not prove that he had never seen an organ, and one might assume that he could know it to be more richly 'harmonious' than other instruments only because he had heard one. Again, however, what he is saying is likely to be hearsay, the words of a Saxon poet, no more concrete than when a nineteenth-century English poet speaks of lyres and dulcimers.

Nevertheless, while recognizing the poem's musical vocabulary as something familiar from other poets or encyclopaedists like St Isidore of Seville (†636) – words such as *cithara, psallebat, modulamine, modulor, carmina, chordae, pulso, cantus* – one could nevertheless find the picture 'real', for the sound of the organ is loud (less meagre than strings) and its looks are luxurious (gilt or golden). Even then, however, that

---

[4] In Lapidge & Rosier: 104, the last line is translated 'even though other songs glitter with gilded surfaces', but *auratis capsis* sounds like a reference of some kind to organs: Aldhelm is commenting on both the looks and the sound of the 'instrument with bellows'.

organs were larger than other instruments is already clear from one of the best-known and authoritative books in the Christian canon, the same commentary of St Augustine. In connection with Psalm 56, Augustine defines the organ as an instrument:

quod grande est, et inflatur follibus.	that is large and blown with bellows.
(PL 36.671)	

Augustine also discusses the organ in relation to *cithara* and voice, perhaps prompting other ideas in Aldhelm's lines.

In his thirteenth *Riddle*, Aldhelm speaks of the organ again, now singing a hundred songs (*centenos cantus* – MGH AA 15.2.103) while voice and strings are silenced:

me praesente stupet vox musica chorda fibrarum.
in my presence the musical voice and string of gut are struck dumb.

In this he could be both describing something he had heard and paraphrasing the psalm-commentaries. But which of the following is more likely? – that Augustine knew organs and had heard them being played in great Mediterranean cities in *c.*400, or that there were vestiges of Roman pipe-technology (even actual Roman organs) surviving in the settlements and primitive monasteries of Aldhelm's England in *c.*700? Surely the former. For centuries after his death Augustine taught his northern readers about Mediterranean Christianity, not least the performance of psalms in an old, distant and foreign religion.

Aldhelm's words 'gilt chest' lead to some rather different conjectures. What extant examples there are of late Roman and early Saxon metalwork prove that fine techniques and materials were known to some early Christians in England,[5] so it is faintly possible that Aldhelm did know an actual organ with a chest of gilt copper or gold-leafed wood. The chest of later Byzantine organs was golden, as was many a *capsa* of another kind in Western abbeys, i.e. *capsa* meaning 'a reliquary'. One oddity in Aldhelm's lines, however, is that he

---

[5] e.g. the Mildenhall treasure or the find of late Roman vessels from Water New-ton, some with Christian chi-rho symbols (British Museum).

does not refer to pipes, either with familiar words like *fistula* (used by St Jerome †420 and St Gregory †604) and *calamus* (used by Cassiodorus †c.585), or with unfamiliar or archaic words. In view of his other technicalities (references to cithara strings, the plectrum, full bellows) one might expect him to make some unambiguous mention of them. Shining bronze pipes or golden trumpets are spoken of by antique authors,[6] and one wonders if the poem meant by *capsae* the gilt pipes themselves, sitting on the chest? While the word means organ-chest in Wulfstan's tenth-century poem (see chapter 5), one cannot be sure it does in Aldhelm. Why use the word in the plural?

In leaving such uncertainties as these Aldhelm is a typical example of the well-read Christian poet. Much the same may be said of the early authors of Spanish (Mozarabic) hymn-texts, who, however, do appear to use the word *organa* concretely, referring to actual instruments and not merely developing symbols and allegories. Symbolic or concrete, however, what early writings were doing was keeping the idea of organs alive through impoverished centuries when few people knew them. At certain moments and in certain instances, evidence of actual instruments (or what seems to be such) does surface, and most of it is summarized in the following chapters. But in any case, before, during and after these outcrops of concrete information writers were continuing to speak of organs, and some scribe-artists were even attempting to draw them.

Byzantine Organs

The references to organs in the *Ceremonial Books* and other documents from ninth- and tenth-century Constantinople so recall practices of late imperial Rome as to offer a picture of how things were in Rome itself.[7] Organs were played at diplomatic receptions and in palace ceremony, at banquets and weddings, at the hippodrome or out of doors at state arrivals (*adventus*), and at various royal events in connection with

---

[6] e.g. Claudian and Athenaeus, in Perrot 1965: 383, 374.
[7] The references from which extracts are given here appear in full in Schuberth: 56–93.

church festivals. Organs were also feats of technology and the decorative crafts, impressing visitors and serving as items of show for the benefit of both the Franks and the Arabs, mechanical wonders comparable to the nearby clock in St Michael that struck the 'church hours'.[8] Although the two main questions that might now be asked – what kind of instrument were the organs (what was their sound like?) and what precisely were they used for (what did they play?) – cannot be answered, the various references to them give some idea of both.

For events and ceremonies in the hippodrome of Constantinople the *Ceremonial Books* mention the imperial organ *(basilichon organon)*, but it would be a mistake to see its sounds and signals as mere circus noise. Imperial ceremony was as sacred as it was secular, and a distinction between the two would not have been made in this connection. Thus while it is unknown whether the *organon* played disordered screeching noises or a properly ordered melody *(modulatio)* and even chords *(organum)*, one can assume it gave a sense of occasion, perhaps instilled awe. Though movable, even portable, its sound must have been strong: one advantage of the water-organ is that for a given wind-pressure its wind-raising apparatus could be less cumbersome than that of a bellows-organ, and smaller and more reliable.

In the case of the fourth-century obelisk of Theodosius, however, it seems to be an organ with bellows that is participating in the orchestra.[9] The bellows are trodden by two boys or slaves, and a capacious windtrunk curves upwards to a chest which is deep enough for several ranks. An alternative interpretation would be that the boys are standing on a wind-regulator (like the bag of a bagpipes) to make steady and constant the wind raised in some other way not seen. The obelisk was erected in 390 in the hippodrome itself, and it pictures various circus scenes, including the royal entourage, other instruments (syrinx, aulos) and dancers, all very symmetrical. Such symmetry was more a graphic symbol of the

---

[8] According to Liutprand of Cremona's report of the year 919, edited in Becker: 90 *(ecclesiasticarum horarum)*.
[9] The obelisk panel, reproduced in e.g. Perrot 1971: plate IV, apparently shows two organs to the left and right, but these could be interpreted as the same object in a panoramic view.

emperor's divine position, one imagines, than a representation of the actual *mise-en-scène* in the hippodrome.

Each of the Byzantine court factions, the Blues and the Greens, had its organ participating in processions when they acclaimed the bride at state weddings. These may have been the so-called silver organs from the palace, part of the extensive grounds of which – gardens, fountains, atria, halls – were open for a variety of processions of the sacred-secular kind. The Golden Hall of the palace had its golden organ, but in neither of these instances is it clear how many organs there were, which (if not all) were portable, and what the terms *silver* and *gold* meant – solid panels or revetments as on reliquaries of the period, with silvered or gilt pipes? The organs seem to have been rebuilt or replaced from time to time. The Emperor Theophilos (829–42) also had a golden or gilt tree in which wind-activated mechanical birds may have sung. They would have been part of a battery of gilt automata placed around the throne in the Great Hall, including a growling lion that sounded at certain moments in a latter-day imitation of the throne of Solomon as described in 2 Chronicles 9. Assuming that all this apparatus worked by wind-power, more likely than banks of bellows supplying the wind would be a pair of hydraulic pistons-and-cylinders located beneath the throne-room.

From the descriptions in the *Ceremonial Books* and elsewhere a certain picture of organs can be built up (Schuberth: 56f, 68ff, 74f):

> on a platform in the reception hall of the palace stood a golden organ *(chrysoun organon)* on one side, a throne on the other, with a cross between the two. The emperor came in to sit on the throne and organ-sound was heard at certain moments, related in some way to the moving of the curtains (as a Veil in the Temple? – see *Ceremonial* of 838);

> in the Great Hall (the same?), there was a golden organ between pillars on the right side, placed outside draped curtains; beyond it was the Blues' silver organ, opposite which was the Greens' (– report of the reception of Saracen representatives in 946);

> in the Clock Room were two golden organs of the emperor and two silver organs of the factions *(ibid.)*;

in the Hall of Justinian the throne was on a tribune below
which stood two silver organs and their blowers *(argura
organa . . . aulounta)*, behind (or in front of?) two curtains
(– *Ceremonial* of 957).

The first of these was imposing enough to be called 'the chief
wonder' *(protodauma)*, but whether any of these instruments
were automata – playing automatically when the wind was
raised – is not clear, despite recent claims that all such early
organs were no more than this (see Hammerstein). Better
detail on the organs is provided in a further Arabic report of
a banquet in the ninth century:

> an organ is brought in and set up: it has a central wooden part
> like an oilpress, covered in leather and carrying sixty copper
> pipes plated in gold. Three 'crosses' are brought in and fitted.
> Bellows 'like smiths' bellows' are then fitted into one side, and
> two men blow while a third plays.

Not the least interesting detail is the 'crosses': these could
have been some kind of framework of timber, fixed to hold
or keep steady the bellows and their trunk, perhaps including beams for the blowers to hold on to. Some such bellows-
frame is also implied in the twelfth-century treatise of
Theophilus, not for an organ but for a forge (see below,
p. 124). The artist of the Utrecht Psalter (see below, p. 108)
may also have known about such frameworks, hence the
cross-like frame he drew above the chest of his organ, if not
actually around the pipes themselves.

Arabic Organs

Even less is certain about details of Arabic organs, and yet
early references in Arabic books on engineering or musical
theory do give some details of them. Two descriptions under
the name Muristos survive from medieval sources, and
although little is clear about either their author or how they
come to exist at all, it seems likely that they derive ultimately
from Greek accounts concerning Ctesibius (see above, p. 19).
In their present form, they may belong to much the same
period as the copies of Vitruvius in Carolingian Europe.
There was clearly a body of technical literature circulating in

the eastern Mediterranean over at least the first Christian millennium, but so far its origins and lines of transmission, at least as they affect musical instruments, have not been explained, nor is it likely that they ever will be.

The sources[10] aim at summarizing two organ-types. One uses a whole skin in which the wind is collected and regulated and from which a conical duct feeds three linked, airtight skins or chest-sections. On each chest sit four pipes, whose length is in the proportion of $x:2x:3x:4x$. Some form of valve controls the wind to the pipes, perhaps a key-action of some kind, although no keyboard as such is described. Perhaps in accordance with interest in the ancient modes of music in Hellenistic-Arab lands, there is also a description of the different moods or effects produced by different combinations of notes. In the nature of so much in early technical treatises, what the description seems to offer is not directions for making apparatus but a generalized account of what such apparatus could contain, what a craftsman should aim for. This would depend on his way of making the various necessary parts, and for this no advice or directive is offered.

The three skins on which the pipes sit are a good example of how a technical treatise conveys aim and function rather than method. Here the author is showing a principle of construction in which a divided chest can be made airtight and its sections given equal wind-pressure by inflexible brass tubes passing between them. No further detail is given, but the principle – something for the craftsman to work out in his own way – is clear. Similarly, 'twelve' pipes in such arithmetic proportions are likely to be only a token number, as therefore would be their length-ratios and presumably their combinations. Finally, other than a reference to the organ's solid base, the rigid framework that would be required to hold it all together is not described, presumably because carpentry work was not the stuff of engineering treatises. But the organ surely needed such a framework.

Even this free interpretation may be overestimating how 'realistic' such a treatise was meant to be. In the West, a similar Eastern organ was described in the so-called *Letter of St*

---

[10] These remarks are based on Farmer: 62ff and 127ff.

Jerome to Dardanus (PL 30.219f), probably one of the ninth century's 'forgeries'. It was said to be a signal instrument on the Mount of Olives in Jerusalem, with a penetrating sound, twelve bronze pipes, a pair of elephant skins for the chest, and twelve or fifteen bellows. One Western commentator of the ninth century understood all this as no less than an allegory for the gospel, its message spread by the twelve apostles 'making a loud sound' (PL 111.496f). In any case, far from supporting each other the *Letter to Dardanus* and the Muristos treatise could be variants of some common fund of cryptic technical information, neither justifying the assumption that such instruments were ever known in Palestine and other Arab lands. Will it ever be certain that they were?

The same question can be asked about the other organ described by Muristos: a loud siren in which wind is fed into a water-chamber, where it is compressed and sent on to blow one or more (four, five) pipes. How it was to be fed is unclear, but it was probably from three round metal cylinders of the kind indicated by Vitruvius or Hero. The single pipe of such a siren, presumably some kind of reed, could be very large, alone or with its chest some six metres (!) high. To make this roar, the wind-pressure in the bronze cistern must have been as great as was feasible before the advent of steel cylinders.

Whatever the actuality of some of these reports of Byzantine and Arabic organs, there is an important factor common to all of them. They were associated with rulers or representatives of political or military power, not with churches themselves, monasteries or religious life in general. Neither the Byzantines nor the Muslims ever came to use organs in their usual services. Nor is there any indication that the crafts and technologies involved in making organs or sirens were available at all outside the workshops of those men in power.

The Court of the Christian Franks: Pippin

In 757, a few years after Pippin, King of the Franks, had been publicly acknowledged on Frankish soil by the pope, and had asked Rome for teachers to bring liturgical texts and show the clergy how to sing them (see also chapter 3), the Eastern Emperor in Constantinople dispatched to him one of the teams of envoys that quite frequently passed between Eastern and Western rulers.

As successors to (some might say usurpers of) the Merovingians, the Carolingian kings understood perfectly well the power of the written word. Even more than their predecessors, they aimed to develop reliable documentation for at least some of their acts,[11] not only matters concerning law and property but also certain events that took place during their reigns. One of the recorded events was the arrival of the Byzantine envoys, recorded by annalists as a token that their king was accepted by the emperor. More than twenty annals, most of them copied long after the event, refer to the organ included in the Byzantine gifts of 757, and although it looks as if successive copyists glossed the details, it would only be true to the nature of such records that such copyists made out the original event to be noteworthy.[12]

They record that in the year 757 (or 756) an *organum* (or *organa* or *organo musico*) was sent to Pippin by Constantinus, the Roman emperor in the East (*rege grecie*), and that with other gifts it arrived in *Francia* from Constantinople (*de graecia*). Technically, Constantinus was still the Roman emperor while the pope who was said to have crowned Pippin was only bishop of Rome, so the gift was of some significance. Various of the annals record that Pippin was then in convocation at the people's assembly at Compiègne, that it was the year in which the emperor made his peace with the Franks, and that the organ was otherwise unknown by them (*antea non visum fuerat in francia*). It is not difficult to see the last two claims as in some way connected: the gift was a unique token of the emperor's acknowledgement of the Carolingians, and before he made the gift the organ was unknown in the West and would have remained so if he had not.

It is the claim that the *organum* was not otherwise known that has misled so many later historians, for what these annals are recording has no bearing on churches or monastic life. Although the emperor very likely knew of Pippin's interest in

[11] Hence too, perhaps, the stimulus towards musical notation already in Charlemagne's time.
[12] The items given in Perrot 1965: 394–5 and Schuberth: 114–16.

establishing chant and his own *cappella* to serve as a model for the correct way of singing it in the West, nothing in the life of his own Byzantine churches and monasteries would have caused him to associate organs with such things. His gift was not for Pippin's churches or for church services except in so far as, if it accompanied the king on his progresses (like trumpets for the later kings of England), it could conceivably have been with him when he entered the modest chapel at Compiègne or at any other of his *villae*.

The very ambiguity of the word *organum* is interesting here, for although more than one later annalist tried to clarify it with such terms as *organo musico*, it is not unlikely that originally it meant not an 'organ' of any familiar kind but some special mechanical device such as a siren. *Organum* could be an 'apparatus' with pipes speaking on a high pressure and making a noise very different, one imagines, from church music. The instrument (called *organon* by the visiting envoys?) would have signalled the king's presence or even accompanied him on military campaigns. One copy of the Arabic treatise of Muristos referred to above even speaks of such a hydraulic siren being made for the 'King of the Inner Franks'.[13] In any case, however, the chroniclers' words are unreliable, for the very phrase 'never seen or heard before' was something of a formula.[14]

Such problems make it clear that we will never know what Pippin's *organum* was, but two other things are reasonably sure. First, most of the annalists probably did not know either, and would assume it was something special; second, and more importantly, annals were not the place in which there would be a mention of any ordinary instruments *(organa)* possessed by the very monasteries in whose scriptoria these annals were being copied. A copyist writing not only some time after events but by then aware that some monasteries had organs, could read his sources in various ways. Annals were something to be unthinkingly copied, something to be interpreted and glossed if need be (so *organum* becomes

[13] Texts and discussion of such questions in Farmer: 150ff.
[14] In the *Fredegar Chronicle* it was used about another significant gift to a Carolingian monarch: Pope Gregory III's presentation of relics of St Peter to Charles Martel in 739 (Wallace-Hadrill 1960: 6). But Petrine relics had already circulated, not least in England.

35

organum musicum), and something that answered questions puzzling to the copyist himself, namely, how did his monastery come to have an organ and who had the first one?

The Court of the Christian Franks: Charlemagne and Louis

Other kinds of question can be asked about the next written reference to organs in the West. The *Life* of Pippin's son Charlemagne, written well after his death, probably by Notker Balbulus, a monk of St Gall (†912), says that another Byzantine legation came over in 812 and brought with it to Aachen 'all kinds of instruments' *(omne genus organorum)* among which was 'that very special instrument of the musicians' *(illud musicorum organum praestantissimum)* which had bellows and a range of sounds from rumbling thunder through chattering lyres to charming bells (MGH SS 2.751).

While it is entirely possible that there was a second Byzantine organ or siren at the Court of the Franks, this is the only reference to it. It might just bear on the question of what had happened to the king's father's *organum* of 757: was it still in use? More likely, however, is that Notker is mingling snippets of information picked up from various sources: ambiguously worded annals in his library, the report of an Islamic legation in 806, the tales of the homage paid to Charlemagne by various Eastern leaders (reports in MGH SS 2.451–2), references to bellows in the psalm-commentaries, references to the three ranges of music (low–middle–high, or thunder–lyres–bells) in poems or other literary sources, and even concrete details of an actual organ he had learned about or knew personally.

The last is questionable, for although some kind of organ may have been known at St Gall by *c*.900, Notker refers to *doliis ex aere* ('vessels of bronze', or 'vessels filled with wind') as if he thought a bellows-organ would have the cylinders or cistern of a water-organ. This is not only unlikely in itself (though in theory bellows could as well feed the cistern as pumps) but would also suggest that Notker's information came more from books than from personal experience at St Gall or anywhere else. Similarly, if *doliis* means not the cistern but the chest, one wonders why the plural is used and whether the reference is any more real than Aldhelm's *capsae* two centuries earlier (see p. 26–8). On the other hand, none of this proves St Gall did not have an organ in Notker's time: it would be nothing new for a monk-scribe to rely on written information for something he could easily have described in his own words from an actual example.

Virtually the only thing one can be sure about is that if there was an organ of 812 at Aachen, it too had nothing to do with the chapel or its regular liturgy except in so far as both organ and chapel belonged to the king. But since there would have been occasions on which the king, perhaps in his balcony on the west front of the chapel, was present at celebrations that included more or less formal ensemble music (*organum*) sung by the *cappella*, this may say more than at first appears. In fact, one recent answer to how the organ came to be a church instrument has centred on the very possibility that the Frankish kings did use organs (presumably the Byzantine gift in the first instance) as royal accoutrements. Originally 'an instrument of the imperial court-music', it somehow 'found its way into the inside of Frankish churches', and from there, 'evidently in the train of Benedictine reform', was 'taken over into English churches' in the tenth century (Holschneider 1968: 142).

Unfortunately, there are various problems with this explanation. In the first place, there is no concrete clue at all about how such an imperial emblem could find its way into churches, and one would rather imagine that it was kept exclusive to the king's person, like a sceptre or like the golden organ in Constantinople. Even if it did find its way in, a question would be: Did it stay? And in the second place, if it is so that organs became familiar to Anglo-Saxon Benedictines (such as those at Abingdon and Winchester) only from their connections with Frankish churches, where were they in the nearly two centuries that separate Aachen in the year 810 from Winchester in 990?

The third and final Carolingian court-organ reported on in documents, this time associated with Charlemagne's son Louis the Pious, does not contribute much new to the story. According to several good sources[15] a Venetian *presbyter* Georgius was brought to the court in 826 (probably then sitting at Ingelheim, near Mainz) and said he could make an

---

[15] MGH SS 1.214, 1.359, 2.513, 2.629f and 15.1.260, given in Schuberth: 122f.

organ in the Byzantine style *(in more graecorum)*. Louis sent him to Aachen with authorization to acquire what he needed since it was something not in use previously *(ante se inusitata)*, whereupon Georgius made the organ *(hydraulica)* with skill and placed it in the palace or hall at Aachen *(in aquensi palatio . . . aula)*. This equipment was something the Greeks had been proud of, and since it had not appeared in Francia before, it would now serve as a warning for the Greeks to submit to the Frankish yoke.

Again, there is little question here of any church organ. Even a court rhetorician could not imagine that a few ranks of copper pipes placed in the Aachen chapel-gallery more than a thousand miles away would make the Byzantines quake with fear. But a powerful military siren, and what it stood for, might. If the two 'genuine' Carolingian organs were high-pressure hydraulic sirens, they would have been useful both as a tactical signal in battle and, more subtly, as a demonstration in diplomatic circles that a difficult technology had been mastered by the Franks. Furthermore, as a royal emblem it signalled legitimacy for the Frankish king much as it did for the Byzantine emperor.

On the other hand, if the *organa* were more chamber-like instruments, comparable to those in the reception hall at Constantinople (see above, p. 3), they must have had similar courtly purposes, again linking the two rulers. Since such instruments cannot have been too large, it seems unlikely that they and their sound would never enter one or other of the churches in these Christian cities, if only because for the rulers themselves there can have been no break between their sacred and their secular acts. However, this would still not make these instruments 'church organs', even if they did eventually appear in monasteries for comparable reasons – as a signal for the people and as wonderful mechanisms to inspire awe, if not for the king then for the King of Kings.

Documents give only the vaguest hints of how Louis's organ was used, and none whatever to link it to any liturgy, regular or ceremonial, as would be expected had it been heard on such occasions. One might think at first that when Walahfrid Strabo, a courtier-poet resident in Aachen 829–38, wrote some obscure verse about a woman actually dying from the sweetness of sound coming from an *organum* (MGH

Poet lat 2.374), he was describing some kind of event in, say, the palace courtyards. But just as likely is that he was alluding to traditional tales about sound's miraculous powers, negative or positive, over its hearers. There are contemporary Arabic reports of hearers dying from frenzy at the sound of a siren (see Farmer), and it would not be surprising if Walahfrid knew the Sirens' scene in the *Odyssey* as translated and interpreted by Cicero in *De finibus* 5.

While the Sirens may seem more appropriate to Walahfrid's phrase 'sweetness of sound' (*vocum dulcedine*) than a military siren does, it would also be true that a siren of four or five pipes as described in the Arabic sources would create sweet melodic phrases if the pipes could be played separately and their intonation was steady. A succession of in-tune sounds is by definition melodious, and the four or five notes would allow many a psalm-tone to resound through the courtyards of Aachen. Also, one cannot be certain that Vitruvius's architectural treatise, known in Aachen during Charlemagne's reign (see p. 18), had not aroused interest with its description of a water-organ – perhaps even sufficiently so for leading men of the court to respond to the priest Georgius's claim that he could make one if he had the right materials.

To exactly the same period as Georgius's organ and Walahfrid's poem, both apparently created for the Emperor Louis, belong the pictures of two hydraulic organs in the Utrecht Psalter (see p. 108), one of them for the King David of the Psalms, with whom Louis was compared by contemporaries. One is bound to wonder what is the significance of three very different types of documentation (biography, poem and drawings) all being produced in the Frankish homelands about, or concerning events about, the year 830. Is the Psalter's drawing based on Georgius's *hydraulica*? If so, does it derive from the instrument itself or, more likely, from a written account of it? Considering how rare at this period are references to any kind of instrument, there does appear a constellation of material here. But whatever the truth, one thing stands out: none of them need have had anything to do with the regular church liturgy, even if in their different way both the Emperor Louis and King David were sacred persons.

3

Organs as Church Instruments

The Question

How the organ came to be a church instrument is a question that has been occasionally asked in the past, but on the whole music-historians have rather taken the situation for granted: the organ was always there, or a particular saint or king introduced it, or a particular pope authorized it, or it came from the Arabs and/or from the Byzantines. Furthermore, it did not appear in any particular church before documents actually mention it, when of course it was used for music in the service.

None of this is likely to be true. The problem is that not everything is one hundred per cent demonstrably untrue, for the story is not simple, there are many strands in it, and 'evidence' as now normally understood does not exist, perhaps never did. Only a few hints and a few potentially misleading references in extant sources give a glimpse of practices across a continent in the course of a millennium and more. The question itself would occur to writers only when they began to enquire about the origin of man-made objects or local customs, which was unusual during the key centuries 750–1250. A hint of the spirit of enquiry to come is found during this period in the cumulative *Book of the Popes* (*Liber pontificalis*), in which various popes are claimed to have introduced or authorized such objects as patens or chalices, i.e. other sacred equipment used in Western Christian practice and needing proof that it is there legitimately.

By the thirteenth century writers are making a habit of remarking on the presence of the organ, and doing so in some such terms as these:

et hoc solo musico   and this is the only musical
instrumento utitur ecclesia . . . instrument the church employs,

propter abusum histrionum,	
eiectis aliis	. . . the other instruments
communiter instrumentis.	having all together been banned because of abuse by play-actors.

(GS 2.388)

The words attributed here to the Franciscan Ægidius Zamorensis (Gill of Zamora, †c.1320) follow on the definition of an organ taken from St Augustine, and were found in writings elsewhere. They need not mean that an author using them knew organs any more than did writers who referred to organs allegorically, such as the reformer Gerhoch, an Augustinian canon of Reichersberg (†1169):

Tota ecclesia est	The whole church is
organum dei,	the organ of God,
electi sunt	the elect are
fistulae dulcisonae.	sweet-sounding pipes.

(PL 194.500)

Such allegory, based on the psalm-commentaries, matches Scripture's accounts of practices in the Temple of the Old Testament and may say little about what actually happened in twelfth-century Augustinian collegiate churches. In the first place organs serve as Christian versions of the sacred Jewish instruments; and in the second they are symbols, or physical manifestations, of a harmonious community of believers. Although neither of these writers is dealing with the question of how organs got introduced, together after the event they do produce a reason why some or many major churches had them.

Both Franciscans and the Augustinians may have had particular reasons for ruling on what was and what was not appropriate for their reformed church-practice, including the question of which instruments if any were suitable for playing in church. By the fifteenth century two further kinds of explanation for organs being there emerge. One is based on the pious legends of saints, the other on scholarly examination of papal documents, and both are instructive about the story as a whole.

Emblem of a Saint

Since the fifth-century *Passio* or account of her suffering, St Cecilia like St Agnes had been associated with *organa* and with the inner music of the soul. Mattin texts for Cecilia's name-day, 22 November, include these words from the *Passio* (see Connolly), concerning the impending marriage forced upon her:

cantantibus organis	as instruments [?] were sounding
illa in corde suo soli	she in her heart alone
domino decantabat.	sang to the Lord.

A vespers text omits the second line, implying that Cecilia sang to the organ – exactly what the *Passio* was not saying. Rather, it was showing her to be indifferent to the instruments (? – *organa*) that had been gathered for her marriage to a pagan. This 'indifference' is an old theme: in Psalm 70/71 David is indifferent to the instrument he had made, and sang to the Lord with his own mouth. When by the fifteenth century saints were generally accompanied in representations by simple emblems of their martyrdom, Cecilia was shown holding an organ, but this need not necessarily mean that she played or admired it any more than St Catherine played or admired the wheel on which she was broken. Nevertheless, the image of Cecilia with an organ must have been powerful for two particular reasons.

First, whereas by the fifteenth century an organ would hardly strike anyone as the emblem of a saint's suffering, virgin martyr or not, people in the early Christian centuries would easily have seen *organa* as a signal for her violation. All around the Mediterranean early Christians were familiar with the licentious sound of instruments at wedding feasts, especially in the charivari-like carousing associated with these events. Since in the big cities people also knew organs in arenas, such an instrument would stand both for pagan ceremony and for the coercion of Christian believers – in the amphitheatre or bridal chamber, as the case may be. Even if northern Europeans were not so familiar themselves with the part it played in pagan weddings, the better read would have been familiar with St Jerome's advice to Christian virgins to be deaf to *organa* and to 'songs of the world' (*cantica mundi* – PL 22.875, 871).

Second, because the fifteenth century was a period when organs could have been found in most major and not a few minor churches, when the greatest churches had several of them, and when their formal music could have been heard as a regular part of services or even (here and there) recitals, to associate it with a long-dead saint would be a justification for its presence after the event. Associating the organ with Cecilia was a little like associating the chant itself with another inspired and lamented saint, St Gregory. An organ would also be a Christian emblem, parallel to the traditional harp of David, king of the Israelites and creator of the Psalms. (This harp of medieval painters and sculptors also hangs on a mis-understanding, however.) It might not be an explanation of why the organ had come to be there, but it would help make it legitimate when it had.

Naturally, there is guesswork in any such account, not least since it is still by no means clear how much earlier than the fifteenth century Cecilia was associated with organs in pictures. It is striking that the earliest writers of books on musical instruments, such as Arnolt Schlick and Sebastian Virdung (both in 1511), no more refer to St Cecilia than do the earlier medieval treatises that dealt with the calculation of organ pipe-lengths. Authors engaged in such scientific researches had no need of pious explanations for something whose presence they did not query in the first place.

As well as all this, however, there is a more basic problem with the story of St Cecilia: in the earliest texts, *organis* may not have meant 'organ' at all, or even 'instruments in general'. Not only may Cecilia have been indifferent to instruments and the lewdness associated with them at pagan weddings, but she may have been indifferent to all music and all sung liturgy. The text of the legends would not refer to her singing *musica*, since one did not use the word 'music' in this way – *ars musica* meant the theory of notes and their study. But an early legend might refer to her hearing *organa*, and *organa* could mean one of several things: ensemble music performed with other voices and instruments; the unison chant set for the various texts in the order of matrimony; perhaps the words of the liturgy themselves (for *organum* meaning the mass and daily services, see p. 55); even just 'music'.

Generally, one could say that in non-technical texts such as those sung in a liturgy (including those for 22 November), there seems no reason to translate *organum* as 'organ'. Not for centuries would various texts referring to Cecilia – not, e.g. the tenth-century *Benedictional of Æthelwold* – associate her with music in any way. Nor do later representations, such as the twelfth-century tympanum in the church of St Cecilia, Cologne. Only gradually would representations distinguish her from other virgin martyrs, and only gradually would vocabulary change and become more specific. But the fifteenth century, including its painters, would not be aware of any of this, and no one in Raphael's lifetime would have thought that *organis* could mean anything but 'organ'.

Introduced by a Pope?

One history of the popes *(Liber de vita Christi ac omnium pontificum)*, first published in 1474 by Bartolomei Sacchi (known as Il Platina), appears to attribute Pope Vitalian (657–72) with standardizing the chant and admitting organs into church. Widely copied (here from *De vita & moribus summorum pontificum historia*, Rome, 1529, pp. 75–7), the passage reads:

At Vitalianus cultui divino intentus, & regulam ecclesiasticam composuit, & cantum ordinavit, adhibitis consonantium (ut quidam volunt) organis.	And Vitalian, intent on the holy liturgy, composed the ecclesiastical rule [= the daily office], and gave order to the chant, employing the *organa* of those sounding together [?] (as it is said).

Obviously, this is not without ambiguity. But in the absence of any archival document actually showing that Vitalian authorized using organs in church, later historians have generally used Platina's statement as the evidence that he did, commenting on it in various ways.

Thus in *Syntagma musicum*, II (Wolfenbüttel, 1619, pp. 90–1) Michael Praetorius notes that Vitalian only 'approved and confirmed' the use of organs *(approbiret und confirmiret)* and that for a long time they had been used for teaching practical harmony. In a seventeenth-century English translation of

Platina's *The Lives of the Popes* (by Paul Rycault, London, 1685, p. 114), the passage appears as 'introducing Organs to be used with the Vocal Musick', thus offering an interpretation of a particularly awkward phrase found in the original. Many later historians added various other pieces of information, all appearing to believe that the answer to how we have organs in church lay in papal or other documentation, if only one could be sure to have enough of it. Some authors have also pointed out that a particularly authoritative source, the *Book of the Popes* or *Liber pontificalis*, which is generally thought reliable for the seventh century, does not say anything about Pope Vitalian and organs, only that

regulam ecclesiasticam . . .	he preserved the ecclesiastical rule
omnimodo conservavit,	in all kinds of ways,

as one book on the popes puts it (the *Anastasii . . . historia de vitis romanorum pontificum,* Paris, 1649, pp. 51–2).

Alas, the whole story seems to be based on a misunderstanding. Platina relied on earlier Italian historians, notably Tolomeo of Lucca whose ultimate source was the 'Life of St Gregory' of Johannes Hymmonides (*Gregorii magni vita,* c.880). Now this Johannes or 'John the Deacon' was amanuensis to Pope John VIII who, like other popes of the period, encouraged the writing of official histories. Such history celebrated the achievements of previous popes as part of the attempt to establish Rome as the unrivalled source of apostolic power, of authorized liturgy and of the chant to which it was sung. But John the Deacon was surely not speaking of any musical instrument when he wrote, concerning Vitalian:[1]

occidentales ecclesiae ita	the western churches were so
susceptum modulationis	spoiling the received musical
organum vitiarunt, ut	*organum* that
Joannes quidam Romanus cantor	John, a certain Roman cantor
. . . in Britannias a Vitalliano	. . . was sent to the Britons,
sit praesule destinatus.	by Vitalian the pope.
(PL 75.91)	

[1] The sources on which John the Deacon drew probably included the Venerable Bede's history of the English people, with its reference to seventh-century cantors from Rome (see note 4).

It is almost certainly John's phrase *modulationis organum* that connects Vitalian with organs, if not by Platina himself (who may have had no idea what it meant and merely reproduced Tolomeo), then by his later readers, and these up to at least 1965, as for example Perrot 1965: 285.

But a basic question remains about what precisely John meant: surely not some kind of instrument *(organum)*, nor even vocal counterpoint *(organum)*, but most probably the approved chant itself and/or its text. If *organum* was not merely a word for the fixed or *organized* words of the liturgy, which it may have been, it could denote the chant. After all, this was formal melody whose notes were not the untutored sounds of everyday secular music but those of a rational, calculated scale of music (i.e. 'organic', *organicis*). There needed to be a means of referring to the 'white-note scale' as we now know it, and 'organic' was one such term. It is not out of the question that a pope, somewhat after the event no doubt, was expected to acknowledge something so central to church practice as the musical scale to which its chants are sung, one that (as every singer still knows) requires practice to sing in reasonable tune.[2] To attribute the acceptance of this scale and its kind of non-folk, non-pagan, non-barbaric music to Vitalian and his period was plausible.

Curiously, just as there is a certain parallel to St Cecilia in the story of St Agnes, who disdained *organa* for the sake of her Saviour's gifts,[3] so there is a parallel story to Pope Vitalian authorizing organs: in the ninth century, the use of bells was attributed to another long-dead saint, St Paulinus of Nola (†431, see MGH Cap 2.479). *Nola* is a term for bell, and one might suppose the legend to have arisen solely because of this were it not that the southern Italian town of Nola had been known from Roman times for its bronzework and metal-casting. So there is some concrete connection between Nola, cast bronze bells and a celebrated saint. Whether Tolomeo or the *Book of the Popes* had in mind any such concrete connections when they attributed the office-bell to Pope Sabinian (†606), hymns to Pope Gelasius (†496), and the founding of two *scholae* to Gregory the Great (†604), is not known.

---

[2] To 'sing in tune' is itself a function of this literate musical scale.
[3] Acta SS 1863 edn., vol. 2, 715.

The Benedictines and Various Reforms

After the two fifteenth-century approaches to the organ and how it came to be a Christian implement, both of which depend on misunderstandings of earlier sources, it is useful to return to the period when large tracts of Europe were still being converted and many people were seeing churches and hearing Christian music for the first time.

When in 596 Gregory the Great sent St Augustine of Canterbury to 'preach the word of God to the English nation', i.e. the southern Angles ruled by the king of Kent,[4] he can have had no inkling that in such areas there would eventually develop practices very different from those in the eastern and western Mediterranean – from those of the southern Christianity known personally to him and to the other Church Fathers. By the ninth century these newly evolving practices included both the way liturgical texts were sung and the way music was taught for liturgical purposes, neither of which would have been recognized by an earlier southerner such as St Benedict himself (†c.550). In describing St Benedict as 'wisely unlearned' (*sapienter indoctus* – PL 66.126) Gregory appears to reject the idea of grace through study, and yet he inspired the kind of evangelical vigour that would inevitably use literacy and technology to the greater glory of God, should there be other factors to make this desirable – such as the need to keep the interest of new converts.

St Benedict may not have advocated *liberal arts* learning, much less the *mechanical arts* founded on work of the Greeks and Romans; but it was on influential monasteries three hundred years later that the whole development of written technology depended. In the same way, it was through them that musical notation became the crucial factor for new music. And as important as their written studies was the part played by monasteries and individual monks in major political developments. When the Carolingian kings of the Franks were pursuing their aims across the tribal homelands of middle Europe and down into Italy, the Benedictine missionaries – successors of St Augustine of Canterbury in *Anglia*, St Boniface in *Frisia*, St Willibald in *Germania* – must have been

---

[4] Bede, *Ecclesiastical History of the English People*, Book 1, Chapters 23 and 25.

their natural allies, conquering with the gospel as the king's dukes did with the sword.

No doubt it was no sophisticated religious revival that Pippin, King of *Francia*, had in mind when he sent for Roman cantors in 752, only information on how the fountainhead – Rome, the pope and his musicians – conducted the liturgy and what texts it was that they used over the church year. His Merovingian predecessors had also sought authorized material from Rome, as had the Anglo-Saxon Church still earlier, so there was nothing new here. But newly founded monasteries and nunneries, which had always had close personal ties to the ruling families, forwarded the king's desire for *unanimity*: they were unrivalled sources of religious-political authority, as they were for interpreting and writing down history. *Unanimitas* was the word used by Pippin's son Charlemagne for the quality he wanted in his kingdom's religious-political life, a quality rigorously sought in the directive or *Admonitio generalis* of 789, which (on the model of Exodus 31?) actually threatened Saxons with capital punishment if they became lax in their observance.

Further reform was in the mind of Charlemagne's son Louis when he sponsored the Council of Aachen (or Inden) under St Benedict of Aniane in 816, a council whose major aim was to establish the liturgy and its canonic texts, as it still was for the Anglo-Saxon reformers six generations later. Clearly, the early Benedictine missionaries themselves must have played a fundamental part in all such programmes.[5] Energetic, not necessarily celibate and not always cloistered in any obvious sense, these monks played a part in the proceedings that was more practical than might be assumed at first. Though energetically making copies of the authoritative books (gospels, psalters, antiphoners or textbooks for daily service), they were also developing ceremony and, if seldom a deep theology, then practical skills. The result was a monastic life complete with, for example, buildings planned and made on principles particular to northwest Roman Christianity rather than to Syrian, Egyptian, Numidian or Byzantine monasticism.

[5] Further remarks on Pippin's initiative in NOHM; on that of Charlemagne and Louis, in Wallace-Hadrill 1983: 259ff, 229ff.

In the year 800, as the king pushed the pagans back a little farther to the east and north, church missionaries would follow, discarding the old pagan emblems such as sacred trees and replacing them by Christian – the cross, eventually the crucifix. Wooden and eventually stone churches and conventual buildings would replace the holy glades in the pagan forests, described centuries before by Tacitus (*Germania* 9, 38, 43); monks would teach not only literacy and chanting but also eventually bronze-casting, paint-mixing, glass-making, silver-chasing, ivory-carving; and a whole community would enthusiastically exhibit any newly acquired relics of a saint, for these would give it the connection it desired with Christian authority and be a physical link with history.

Wherever it was, a Benedictine base-of-operations in the year 800 or so must have been conspicuous, for in many areas forests had had to be cleared for settlement, and its mission was to be more conspicuous and more open than previous holy sites, to make itself felt in all aspects of life.[6] The people were not excluded from Christian shrines that had replaced the out-of-bounds holy glades of the pagans. A stone building made to unheard-of height, with a set of bronze bells ringing across the clearances, with incense and fragrances of various kinds, with a large candelabrum shining on bishops in gorgeous vestments, and with organized chant inside the mysterious spaces: such an awesome picture can have been created only as various technologies were marshalled for the purpose. It seems hardly coincidence that places in northern Europe later associated with crafts and their technical development – Cologne, Paderborn, Hildesheim, Halberstadt – were centres of early and vigorous conversion.

While the Romans had scattered their craft-production evenly over a vast empire, during the years 750–1000 the crafts centred more on particular missionary abbeys, at least in that part of Europe north of a line from Freising to Tours. In such abbeys kings too had vested interests (as well as close family relations), and it is not difficult to believe that *unanimity* had a technological face. Rival abbeys, themselves centres of important provinces, all looked towards being able to

---

[6] Two useful treatments of this missionary activity from the present points of view are in Sullivan and Parsons.

create wonderful things – high bell-towers, wide stone vaults, cast-metal objects, various pieces of ingenious equipment. Earlier and farther south the situation is less clear since documents are so sparse. But when the 'freelance Irish missionaries' (so called in Sullivan: 710) or the various missions springing from Lyons or Lérins were operating south of that line from Tours to Freising, their monastic centres were seldom associated with the heavier crafts needed for ingenious church equipment.

Yet one hesitates to say that 'northern Europe' was more inventive technologically than 'southern Europe', even if known documentation suggests it. After all, the early Celtic missionaries too had developed the idea of communal work (e.g. in making the land arable) and they certainly had books, vestments and at least small bells. Also, it is striking that two particular Celtic foundations far from Francia – St Gall and Bobbio – did become associated with organs in the main period around 1000. But this was after these houses had been developed by the Benedictines and Cluniacs respectively, and such invigorative Orders were often responsible for the church crafts of the tenth century, either in new monasteries or in the older ones they were reforming (Winchester, Lobbes, Hirsau).

It would not be difficult to imagine special equipment sooner or later being made in these churches and exhibited to the ordinary people *(plebes)* milling in and around them, on feastdays or for regular pilgrimages. The special equipment that increased their wonder in the New Order might include a clock which mysteriously struck a bell at predictable times, a splendid (and mysteriously?) revolving wheel with bells, and an organ playing pipes with wind blown by no man.

The Situation by c.1000

By *c.*1000 evidence is found for various elements in this picture, and while there may be only a handful of references to revolving wheels (Abingdon), organs (Winchester) and some kind of clock (Rheims),[7] it seems likely that workshops

---

[7] Abingdon in RBMAS 2.2.278 (a later chronicle), Winchester in Campbell (Wulfstan's contemporary poem), and Rheims as reported in the twelfth century by William of Malmesbury in RBMAS 90.2.196.

were being set up in many places. Regular written evidence
of such things appears only later.

Reporting on organs in late tenth-century England was a
political-religious act, for the men associated with them were
powerful and their listed achievements stated things about
them. When Bishop Æthelwold (†984) is said to have made
things 'with his own hands' (see below, p. 60), it may or may
not be literally true, for the purpose of the remark was to
show that such a bishop was no longer an aloof aristocrat (he
was shepherd of a flock) and his monastery was no longer a
mere convenience for members of royal families. Similarly St
Dunstan (†988) and St Oswald (†992) were described as giving expensive embellishments to new or reformed monasteries, and in such cases as these the gift was recorded partly
in order to establish its inalienability. To some extent, offering an organ was like offering books (gospels) in earlier
times: both gifts contributed to the liturgy, celebrated the
mission of the Church and remained part of the monastery's
property.

Already in the twelfth century, William of Malmesbury
recognized the reform of English monasteries under St
Dunstan as involving 'great wonders' such as bells and organs
(PL 179.1660). It is also quite possible that organs themselves
were political tokens in so far as such tenth-century reformers as Dunstan and the Anglo-Saxon bishops, or those in the
regions Ghent-Metz and Hirsau-St Gall, may have learned
about the organ brought to King Pippin in 757 and taken as
a sign of Byzantine homage. After all, such events were
reported on in the annals owned by or copied in such monasteries. If for the Carolingian chronicler the gift meant that
his king was recognized by the Eastern Emperor – still offi-
cially the chief Christian power in a period of political pacts
– so for the Anglo-Saxon chronicler the same kind of gift
showed how important his saint was in King Edgar's English
kingdom, in a period of relative peace from the Vikings and
Danes.

For such purposes the sacred and the secular were not
separate. One could not easily say whether the organ was
there for a well-ordered liturgy (summoning and entertaining the people at major events like dedications) or whether it
was there for the splendid occasions when powers of church

and state met together (as they often did in monasteries grand enough to have such equipment). The effect would be much the same, supporting both the divine right of the king and the apostolic authority of the abbot. So it is not surprising that there are various hints that monastic centres in recently converted regions developed the kind of skills that could lead to such things as bells (as in Catalonia) or organ-pipes (as in and around St Gall).[8]

Perhaps some of the technology was brought by travelling craftsmen from Constantinople, where there are tenth-century reports both of ceremonial organs in the court and of a waterclock ringing a bell in church (see chapter 2). But external or exotic influences of this kind have probably been exaggerated by today's historians: the crafts were not so arcane that they could not be locally developed if conditions allowed or if there were demand for them. It is true that work in metal and stone in Catalonia was conceivably helped by skilled men passing across the Arab line into reclaimed Christian areas, just as early contact with Arab teachers in northern Spain probably encouraged the mathematical work of Gerbert of Aurillac, later Pope Silvester II (†1003). But stronger, more consistent and more reliable sources of information of all kinds in c.1000 were more likely to have been those provided by the international Order of Cluniac monks within European Christendom itself. Gerbert, who also became Archbishop of Rheims, was himself in Catalonia because of such connections between abbeys.

The source of Cluniac energies lay in a foundation that might have seemed far away in Burgundy, but it was one that already drew Rome itself into its network. 'Drawing into its network' was physical: the Cluniacs consciously developed a road system for pilgrims and other church travellers, including revenue collectors, across the Alps and Apennines to Rome and (most famous of all) across the Pyrenees and Cantábrica to Santiago. Curiously, however, the early Cluniacs are not known for certain to have had an organ in their greatest abbeys including Cluny itself, although it must

---

[8] Example of bells in Catalonia (Tavara) in Seebass: plate 52; of those elsewhere, in Price: 86ff. On the theory and (perhaps) practice of organ-pipe making in Rheims or St Gall, see pp. 105–8.

have been under their influence south of Rome and south of the Pyrenees that the monastery churches of Cava and Bages were dedicated in splendid ceremonies during which the sound of *organa* was heard (see later in this chapter). Also, Gerbert is known to have involved himself in at least the theoretical side of organs – the calculation of pipe-scales[9] – which may have accompanied actual instruments in the monasteries of Aurillac and Bobbio, and in the cathedral at Rheims (see p. 60). At Cluny some extant carvings on two pier capitals from the ambulatory represent the modes of music and, like the music treatises copied in its monasteries,[10] express the Order's recognition of musical studies. It is also without question that in material wealth, technical knowledge and church-size, the larger Cluniac houses were perfectly capable of making and having a use for organs. The question, then, is whether they did, and if not, why not – what would the absence of organs indicate about the uses to which they were put in those places that did have them?

The Cluniacs' was not an evangelical Order in the manner of the earlier Benedictines, for they tended to move away from physical work and towards a busy liturgical day: it was on their knees and not with their hands that the brothers did the 'work of God', using lay workers for labour and acquiring rents for their more than adequate income. Both in their church architecture and written ordinances the monks kept themselves personally separate from the people, just as the monastery itself claimed papal indemnity against the people's local spiritual leader, the bishop. If, therefore, in Cluniac churches the people did not congregate to celebrate public mass but circulated around the choir or even remained in the Galilee antechurch, and if there was no need to attract the people with wondrous machinery on feastdays – then there was no need for organs. Conversely, where eventually bishop and people did congregate to celebrate public mass, as they did in the secular cathedrals that were

[9] Good summary in Sachs 1980: 171ff and 273ff.
[10] However, both of these areas, and particularly the first – understanding and defining the modes – derived from the teaching of Boethius (†524) and were removed from the practical considerations of cantors or instrument-makers, whether in or out of monasteries.

soon to rise literally above everything else in the new and growing cities, there organs would be found.

Of course, it is always possible that Cluny and other abbeys in the Order did have organs but left no record of them. For they had not yet experienced one other crucial development without which very little would be known about organs even in much later periods: new kinds of concrete documentation. Beginning with records of gifts, fuller documentation gradually included various kinds of fiscal accounts, fabric rolls and eventually organ-builders' contracts. Before then, and in monastic churches less accountable to the public or its representatives, references to organs are much more arbitrary and glancing. Of the written documentation produced in earlier monasteries, even technical literature giving pipe-measurements and (in one celebrated instance) a treatise on making organs does not ever explicitly refer to an actual instrument, although the author probably learned all he knew from it.

The Earliest-Known Church Organs?

While there seems little doubt that the earliest church organs were monastic, it is only by chance that one ever learns of church equipment of any kind: perhaps a few words in the report of a dedication, or in the *Life* of an abbot or pope, or in the legal record of a gift. Seldom would any of these sources of information have any reason to be technical or exact, nor is there any guarantee that the detail they happen to give was typical. There is an additional problem with early references: one cannot be sure that *organum* means the organ, and from time to time historians who have assumed that it does have come to misleading conclusions about 'early schools of organ-building' or 'the origins of organ music'.

Except for that in a well-known book on music-theory (Hucbald, see below),[11] the best-known reference to an *organum* in the late ninth century is found in a letter of Pope John VIII (872–82) to the Bishop of Freising, in Bavaria:

[11] A third celebrated reference to an organ, made by a writer of this period, supposedly concerns events nearly a century earlier: Notker's report of Charlemagne's organ (see above, p. 36).

precamur autem ut	furthermore we pray
	that you either bring or send
	(with the said payments)
optimum organum cum	a very good *organum* with a
artifice qui hoc et moderari	craftsman [?] who can both play
et facere ad omnem	it and achieve all
modulationis efficaciam possit	success in modulation [?]
ad instructionem musice	to instruct us in the [theoretical?]
discipline nobis	discipline of music.
aut deferas cum eisdem	
redditibus aut transmittas.	

(MGH Epist 7.1.287 and PL 126.651)

It is not surprising that many historians have read into this a proof that organs were then in use or at least desired in Rome, that the Bavarians were already expert in organ-making, that things were so developed they were able to send an organist as well, and that the papal *schola* was a place where organ-playing or music theory (probably the latter?) was taught.

Maybe all this is true. But our knowledge of it hangs entirely on the word *organum*, and if this meant not 'organ' but 'a systematic book of chant for the texts of office or mass', then the passage implies something totally different: the pope, in what was a period of desolation and misery in Rome, appealed to one of the northern bishops nearest to Lombardic Italy (one to whom he was already writing for money) for a true copy of the liturgical texts. In addition, he wanted someone who knew how to sing the texts and teach music or modal theory, perhaps with the new notation used in the North and which his cantors had heard about.

This interpretation is much more plausible, and although we would then lose an early reference to 'the organ', it has two good results. In the first place, it very much accords with the idea – already suggested by a variety of evidence – that 'Gregorian chant' was something at first best or only understood by the northern churches, something for the teaching and organization of which a keyboard may have been useful. Even if *organum* did not mean organ but 'some kind of equipment that would demonstrate the musical scale', it would have been useful in Rome. In the second place, it allows for and may explain a striking coincidence, namely that this letter was probably prepared by the papal clerk – the very amanuensis, perhaps – who recorded the passage about Pope Vitalian and his attempts to 'regulate the *organum*' (see above, p. 45). Clearly, chant and the teaching of it were important in later ninth-century Rome.

It is also not unlikely that Italian scribes in particular used *organum* to mean a 'book of authority' such as gospel or psalter. This may have been the case at Canossa in 915 or 951 when a report written later said that the local count gave *organa* in honour of the monastery's saint (MGH SS 31.431). Just as likely as 'an instrument of music' this could mean 'an instrument of liturgy', i.e. a book rather than an organ. In other instances the word would mean something else: the praise *in organis et cymbalis* offered to God when Archbishop Bruno of Cologne was consecrated in 953 (MGH SS 4.259) would have meant 'with bells and instruments', which in turn could include an organ. For the believer, an instrument of liturgy and an instrument of music had a common aim.

In the particular case of Cologne in 953, and in other cases when the document quoted is not contemporary, there is a further possibility arising from the fact that, as one sees with the *organa* of St Cecilia, meaning was not fixed. Since the account of this particular consecration at Cologne was written a century after the event, the author would assume by then that there had been instruments present and would be likely to use an old word-formula such as *in organis et cymbalis* to refer to them.

A particularly striking reference to *organum* occurs in a report of the dedication ceremonies at the Catalonian abbey of S. Benet-de-Bages in 972, for the description is evocative of that kind of festive, noisy event by means of which organs may well have become familiar and acceptable in monastic churches. One would therefore like to be particularly sure what *organum* means. As the priests and the choir praised God,

organumque procul	at a distance the *organum*
diffundebat	poured forth
sonus ab atrio	sound from the courtyard,
laudantes et benedicentes	[all] praising and blessing
Dominum.	the Lord.
(Marca: 898)	

The music is jubilant, there is a crowd of people *(plebes)* present, and the location is out of doors: this is a classic situation for the sound of *organized* ensemble singing and playing. But what is the *organum?* At least three meanings are possible, each of them well documented at the time: ensemble music (including instruments?), vocal polyphony (of improvised or mixed type?), or organ. Viewed in this light, it seems least likely that it means organ, although when the document itself was written some three hundred years after the event – copied or glossed from an original – the scribe may well have thought it did.

For the historian, two particular things follow from the Bages report. In all of these early sources, one should see the word *organum* as versatile (positive) rather than ambiguous (negative). It is a word useful rather than misleading, for if *organum* could mean ensemble music in general, this could be taken to include instruments should circumstances permit. But indeed circumstances did permit when the occasion was jubilant – for public processions, the major feasts, important sacraments (consecration, dedication, matrimony, coronation), indoor or outdoor acclamations for king or bishop – and when the monastery was wealthy enough, as so many of them were by *c.*1000.

The second thing that follows is equally basic: if S. Benet-de-Bages had *organum* at its dedication festival, it seems out of the question that the other major churches of this period in Catalonia did not, even if they were never lucky enough to have a later scribe who left a record of it. Such major churches would be at the very least those of the monasteries of Ripoll, S. Juan-las-Abadesas, Vich, Silos, Montserrat, Cuxa and Canigou. And if Ripoll (the most important) had an organ, then it is hard to believe that by *c.*1000 or so the major reform abbeys north of Catalonia did not too: Cluny, Fleury (see p. 105), Gorze, Brogne, Ghent, Hirsau, Glastonbury and Winchester, to name a few.

Not a single one of these is known from any official church documents to have had an organ. But by a great piece of luck, Saxon Winchester did have a cantor who wrote some verse about its instrument, and both poem and organ may well have been connected with the minster's dedication festivities. This poem deserves a section to itself (see chapter 5) but is useful here as a reminder that knowledge of organs is largely by chance and that Bages and Winchester surely represent a whole bevy of new or reformed monasteries with *organa* of one kind or another, heard at their dedications and no doubt on jubilant occasions afterwards.

Anglo-Saxon Organs

Evidence for organs of some kind in new or reformed monasteries comes from five references in late tenth-century England: at Ramsey, Abingdon, Malmesbury and two successively at Winchester. (For the last, see chapter 5.)

A *Life of St Oswald* reports on events in the year 991 at Ramsey Abbey, and quite uniquely gives four pieces of information about it. First, the local baron

	furthermore
triginta praeterea libras	granted thirty pounds
ad fabricandos cupreos	for making copper
organorum calamos erogavit.	pipes for the organ.

Copper was expensive, and therefore outside the usual run of an average monastery's workshop materials. (What this might suggest about the use of cheaper materials is touched on in chapter 5.) Second, the location of these pipes is described – with some ambiguity, unfortunately for later readers:

qui in alveo suo	which in their cabin [= on their chest? in their enclosed chamber?]
super unam cochlearum	up on one of the spirals [= at the top of a spiral staircase?]
denso ordine	in close-packed rows,
foraminibus insidentes.	sitting on their holes [at the top of the chest?].

Then one learns that the organ was used

diebus festis follium	on feastdays, set in motion
spiramento fortiore pulsati.	by the strong breathing of bellows.

And finally, something is said about the sound and effect of the organ:

praedulcem melodiam et	it emitted very sweet melody and
clangorem longius	strong sound
resonantem ediderunt.	resonant over some distance.
(RBMAS 83.90)	

The situation being described cannot have been unique: Ramsey was not a major abbey compared to Winchester and it can never have had the wealth or significance of Peterborough and Ely nearby. Like others, its new foundation was given a marked attention by the zealous bishops of the time, and in this respect it must speak for a whole crowd of similar foundations in England and Western Europe. Can things have been different in Aquitaine or Saxony?

Some time earlier – thus the first actual organ recorded in England? – St Dunstan (†988) had given *organa* to Malmesbury Abbey, according to a report written a century and a half later by the historian William of Malmesbury:

	[Dunstan was]
offerre crebro.	to make frequent donations.
Inter quae signa sono	Among them were bells outstanding
et mole praestantia,	in tone and size,
et organa . . . per aereas	and an organ [sounding] by means of
fistulas musicis	bronze pipes prepared according to
mensuris elaboratas.	musical proportions.[12]
(RBMAS 52.407)	

Though saying little about the organ – 'bronze pipes' may be formulaic, the words of a well-read scholar – William's account makes it clear that the Malmesbury organ was dedicated to a saint (placed near his altar in the public southeast corner of the church?), that it was a 'wonder' (thus an offering to God and the people), something used in festivals (the reference to this is in RBMAS 83.301–2) and something inalienable: it was a gift not to be moved. This last suggests not so much that the organ was small and too easily removed but that, on the contrary, it was a major part of the abbey's endowed property.

---

[12] 'Prepared according to musical proportions', i.e. *organically* – a term cognate with *organum* in Pope John VIII's letter quoted on p. 55, and in various other early references.

A later report concerning the third of the Anglo-Saxon organs – at tenth-century Abingdon, home of Æthelwold before he moved to Winchester – says that Æthelwold made it with his own hands (RBMAS 2.2.278). But whether *propriis manibus* means more than that the reformer was known to use his hands in physical work (unlike the new aristocratic Cluniacs who were so busy on their knees) is uncertain.[13] He was also said to have made a bell-wheel, some kind of rotating apparatus to which many little bells were attached. Turned by hand or perhaps by wind raised by bellows, it must have given special effects of sight and sound on festive occasions, in these respects comparable to an organ. Where the Abingdon wheel and organ were placed is not known, but they may have been near the centre of the church: the building was large (some $200' \times 57'$) and seems to have had apses giving a centralized effect at the east end not totally unlike Charlemagne's chapel at Aachen.

William of Malmesbury also attributes St Dunstan with spreading *organa* in England:

illud instrumentum	that instrument
quod antiqui	which the ancients
barbiton, nos organa dicimus	call barbiton and we *organa*,
tota diffudit	he dispersed throughout
Anglia.	England.
(RBMAS 63.257)	

But he may have been confusing what his sources had said: it was the string-instrument the cithara, and not the organ, that was 'called barbiton by the ancients', and William would know the story of Dunstan's mysterious cithara which, by itself and untouched by human hand, had played a certain antiphon melody.[14] There is a question too about what William's sources had said about the organ of Gerbert of Aurillac (†1003), made at Rheims and which, according to William, was a water-organ and still existed 'in that church' (*apud illam ecclesiam* – RBMAS 90.2.196). Was it and did it?

[13] The *Life of St Æthelwold* (c.1000) reported of King Eadred that he too had measured out the plan of the Abingdon church 'with his own hands' (PL 137.89).
[14] St Dunstan in Acta SS Mai 4.329; also in Bridfertus's *Life* (PL 139.1423ff), which frequently mentions liturgical music, gives the cithara story, speaks of Dunstan's filling England with holy doctrine, but mentions no organs.

Did William misunderstand the word *hydraulia* and assume that only such apparatus was complex enough to be worthy of such a famous mathematician? Even if one could answer these questions, there would still be nothing to tell whether the organ was in the church-building itself, whether (if it were) it was used for festive services, and if so, how.

What is really significant about William of Malmesbury's words is that a twelfth-century historian was now saying something about the history of organs: a particular saint (Dunstan) or pope (Gerbert became pope in 999) had introduced them in a particular region, and they had a clear purpose in particular churches. William's language might elegantly allude to older literature but what he is concerned with is a concrete object having practical uses, even a status as legal property. However truly this might reflect the way organs were seen in the ninth or tenth century, it clearly does for the twelfth.

Eleventh and Twelfth Centuries

Annalists, biographers and poets continued to use words in old senses, but more and more concrete details gradually emerge. Thus while in 1061 the word *primum* ('first') in the report of St Ulrich, Augsburg, is unclear, *organum* does seem to mean a church organ, and one with a specified location – the report says Abbot Adalbert

primum organum musicum	placed a first-rate organ of music [or: first, he placed an organ]
in templum posuit.	in the church.
(Buhle: 66)	

On the other hand, in so far as one is free to guess, the description of the dedication ceremonies of 1092 in the *Chronicles of Cava*, seems rather to use *organa* to mean 'instruments in general':

dulcissimi concentus	the loveliest sounds
exaudirentur,	were heard, the
organorum, ac tibiarum	modulations of *organa* and flutes [?]
ad iucundissimum	producing a most agreeable
numerum modulationes.	harmony.
(Acta SS Martii 1.334)	

But 'instruments in general' could, of course, include organs. Despite the ambiguity and archaism in the language (*numerum* for 'harmony'), the reference is useful, describing the effects of both incense and ensemble music at the splendid papal consecration of a Cluniac monastery in the south of Italy. Furthermore, since there also exists a further account of this consecration that makes no reference to *organa* or any music beyond the usual psalm-singing, it seems that we know of it here only by chance – without this one reference we would have no reports of *organa* in the whole of southern Italy and for the whole of this period (see also the remarks on Montecassino, p. 96).

Quite the most important twelfth-century source on organs is the treatise of Theophilus described in chapter 5, but its period was one when every reference to an organ gives some useful detail and suggests that many more organs existed than are now known about. The chance nature of references alone suggests this. Only because the notorious murder of the Count of Flanders in 1127 got reported does one learn that the octagonal chapel of St-Donat, Bruges, had an organ. A chance item in another chronicle, this time at Lobbes in the same Ghent-Brogne region of reformed monasteries, reports an interesting event of 1134: the organ given by a previous abbot 'for use in the divine worship of the church' (*in usum divinae laudis ecclesiae* – MGH SS 21.326) was taken away by the Bishop of Arras, who had it transported to his own church, along with the bells. Without this reference, one would know nothing about any organ in either Lobbes or Arras (St Vaast?). Why valuable assets were purloined in this way is not known, but the incident is probably one in the ongoing warfare between bishops and abbots and gives some idea of why a donor might say his monastery organ was not to be moved.

It would be of particular value to establish that there had been an organ in Lobbes because the church was similar to so many others in the Upper Meuse region, and it is probably safe to assume that word of one organ in a well-knit monastic province is a sign that there were others too. In the case of a more southerly group of Benedictine houses, near Lake Constance, a reference from the period certainly suggests this to be the case. At Petershausen in *c*.1130

Counradus abbas	Abbot Conrad
conduxit monachum	employed a certain monk
quendam nomine Aaron	called Aaron,
presbyterum de Châmberch	priest of Komburg [?],
musicae artis peritissimum	very skilled in the *ars musica*,
qui fecit ei organa	who made him an organ
elegantissimae modulationis	of most elegant modulation,
et constituit ea	and set it up
ad meridianam	in the south
plagam eiusdem basilicae.	aisle of the same church.
Ipse etiam iam antea	Previously he had also made
eiusdem generis instrumentum	an instrument of the same kind
Constantiensi ecclesiae	for the church at Konstanz.
fecerat.	
(MGH SS 20.669)	

Here then two or perhaps three organs in one region are indicated (Constance, Petershausen, Komburg), in a rich reference that gives the names of the commissioner and organ-builder, specifies that the builder was a full monk, says where he came from, and notes the location, even the musical tone, of the organ. The words may carry a hint of how the organ was used (melodies? chant? counterpoint?) and perhaps how older organs had sounded (less refined? less used for melodies?). In any case, it looks as if organ-building was the craft-speciality of a certain monk belonging to one south German Benedictine circuit. So it may have been for the monk Theophilus in more northerly areas at much the same period (see chapter 5).

Among concrete hints conveyed by other twelfth-century references are that organs destroyed in the fires at Freising and Magdeburg Cathedrals in 1158 and 1199 must have been vulnerable where they were located (fixed and no longer portable? with wooden casework?); that in cathedrals some such person as the steward or *cellarius* was responsible for this equipment; and that in general the new town cathedrals were active, perhaps more so than monasteries.[15] The last is also suggested by the activities of the Bishop of Arras at Lobbes (see p. 62). It was another French bishop, Balderich, Archbishop of Dol (†1131), who gave the century's most

[15] Freising in MGH SS 24.322, Magdeburg in MGH SS 23.174.

complete *apologia* for organs when he remarked of the Norman abbey of Fécamp:

illa in ecclesia	in this church
unum quid erat quod mihi	was something that pleased me
non mediocriter complacui . . .	more than moderately . . .
ibi siquidem instrumentum	inasmuch as there I have seen
vidi musicum,	the musical instrument
fistulis aeneis compactum,	composed of bronze pipes
quod follibus excitum	[and] which, excited by
fabrilibus	smiths' bellows, produced
suavem reddebat melodiam . . .	sweet melody . . . so that one
ut quidam concinnentium	might think it a certain massed
chorus putaretur clericorum,	chorus of clerics
in quo pueri, senes,	containing boys, old men
juvenes jubilantes	and youths who
convenirent et continerentur;	came together rejoicing.
organa illud vocabant,	They called this an organ,
certisque temporibus excitabant.	and played it at certain times.
(PL 166.1177)	

His letter suggests an organ of some size, with bronze pipes, forge-bellows and a bright sound *(jubilantes)*. Although it looks as if both organ and choir were producing melody *(melodiam)*, it could be merely that the organ was 'melodious' in a broad sense, not necessarily playing actual chant-melodies.

Balderich justifies the organ as, among other things, a traditional metaphor of man inspired by the Holy Ghost, like other special objects in church. He is aware that some people, having no such thing in their churches, criticize those who have. And while acknowledging that it is no sacrilege to be without them, he points out that if there is an organ present, then it is to be used 'according to the church's customary rites' *(uti ecclesiastica consuetudine* – PL 166.1178), presumably meaning certain times or seasons. When clergymen make such remarks, it always suggests that someone somewhere was doing something else.

Since there was no obvious need to say that organs were not known everywhere, it is possible that as a pastoral leader Balderich was reacting to the latest Cistercian criticisms of gratuitous objects in church. Balderich was well-travelled between the Norman monasteries of Jumièges, Bec, St-Wandrille and Worcester, and it is likely that here and there he had found people criticizing the luxurious objects with which such churches were becoming more and more full. Jumièges (with two major monastic churches) and Worcester (with a complex west-end structure) are not known to have had an organ, but it is probable that they did.

If Balderich was positive about organs, Ailred, Cistercian Abbot of Rievaulx (†1167), was certainly not, in his famous tirade in *Speculum caritatis* of 1141–2:

unde in Ecclesia	why [are there] in the church
tot organa, tot cymbala?	so many *organa*, so many bells?
Ad quid, rogo, terribilis ille	For what, I ask, [is] this fearful
follium flatus, tonitrui potius	bellows-blast, more able to
fragorem, quam	express the crash of thunder
vocis exprimens	than the sweetness of the
suavitatem? . . .	voice? . . .
Stans interea vulgus	Meanwhile the people stand, trembling and thunderstruck, wondering at
sonitum follium,	the noise of the bellows,
crepitum cymbalorum,	the clashing of bells and
harmoniam fistularum	the harmony of pipes.
tremens attonitusque miratur.	
(PL 195.571)	

Ailred also complains about various kinds of singing which, as much as the organ, would make one think that the people were assembled 'not in a place of prayer but in the theatre' (*non ad oratorium, sed ad theatrum*). Such remarks are characteristic of purist reformers of all periods.

And yet despite the effectiveness of his words, it is not clear from them whether Ailred had actually experienced either organs or theatres, whether indeed either were there to be seen or heard in twelfth-century Yorkshire. More likely is that he was merely invoking the Church Fathers and their attitude to the *theatrum* (which is referred to in the same section of the treatise), for much of what he writes recalls the Cistercian rhetoric of St Bernard criticizing church-decoration

(PL 182.914–15). Even the reference to people standing – which seems to give a clear impression of the laity's reaction to organs – recalls a traditional etymology of the word *theatrum* as a place in which people 'stand, watching the games' (*stans . . . spectans ludos* – PL 111.553). Similarly, while it would be useful if Ailred's words described organs and bells playing at the same time, he probably intended something less literal: whatever they did, they were both irrelevant to an unsullied Church.

And yet uncertainty about what *was* the early Christian attitude to instruments – did the early Church have *organa* or didn't it? – could leave Cistercians ambivalent about them. With their technologies, forging and mining interests, the members of this mechanically minded Order could have had organs easily enough, and later on in the Middle Ages they certainly did. But any apparent reference to a Cistercian organ before the fourteenth century is unreliable. And as with the Cistercians in the twelfth century, so with the new orders of friars in the thirteenth: some of Ailred's exact words were used in a sermon attributed to the Franciscan Guibert de Tournai, who would have had similar objections to the organs and the music of the worldly Benedictines, to whom he addressed his strictures (*ad monachos nigros* – Aubry: 59).

Organa *in Various Kinds of Document*

During the twelfth century, the ambiguities of the word *organum* do not disappear. Particularly interesting are the *organis* 'suspended' at York in 1147 when a new Cistercian archbishop was being resisted by the clergy: what was suspended was not the playing of organs but the saying of mass. This was also the case in 1221 when the Bishop of Meaux directed his Chapter,[16] who had offended his authority, with these words:

Vos rogamus ut injuriam . . .	we request that the injury . . .
vindicare nobiscum curetis,	you take care to put right with us.
organa vestra in majori Ecclesia	[We are] suspending your
nostra . . . suspendentes.	services in our larger church.

(Du Cange, under 'Organum')

[16] York: without source in Freeman. Concerning the Bishop of Meaux: see Du Cange, under 'Organum'.

The formula 'to suspend the *organum*' (meaning the official text of services) was one used well into the fifteenth century, by bishops or popes not expert in musical matters.

Writers who were expert had to find ways to make it clear that with the word *organum* they did mean the instrument of pipes and bellows. Hence the use of fuller phrases like *organum musicorum*, or 'the instrument of the musicians'. The opening words of a twelfth-century text originating in a south German monastery and associated with Engelberg Abbey call it 'the organic chorus, the musical instrument':[17]

Audi chorum organicum	listen to the organic *chorus*,
instrumentum musicum	the musical instrument
modernorum artificum . . .	of up-to-date artists [craftsmen?],
cantum perfice doctis	play the *cantus* with trained
digitis sonum musicae	fingers, a musical sound with
neumis placitis . . .	pleasing tones . . .
choro chorus accinat	let chorus sing with chorus in the
diaphonico modo et organico.	style of diaphony and *organum* [?].

Even this is not free of ambiguity, however. Although generally taken to be a description of organ-playing, in church and on a keyboard with finger-keys, the conventional musical-poetic terms in the poem make one wary of seeing any technical information in it. Perhaps the organ was actually playing a melody (*cantum perfice*) as well as ensemble music (*diaphonico, organico*), but *chorus* could mean a group of secular musicians as much as a monastic choir. It is also tempting to assume that the note-by-note letters added above the words of the first seven lines in the Engelberg copy of the poem:

Example 2

added letters:

F E D C   F G A F   F E D C   D F F

interpreted as:

[17] The text is that of a conductus or 'instrumental sequence' complete with san-gallian neumes (musical notation as developed at St Gall) in the Engelberg copy, one of six sources. In Dreves 21.204. The place of origin for the poem may have been St Blasien, another south German Benedictine house.

are the notes played by an instrument. On this basis the Engelberg manuscript is often said to carry 'the oldest piece of organ music'. However, there is no necessity to see a poem about organs as something performed on or with an organ, at least a full church organ. The secular rhythms of such a text suit a secular instrumental ensemble, and it is difficult to imagine any opportunity in the liturgy itself for such a poem in praise of church organs.

However, other twelfth-century poems do evoke organs in church. In the *Roman de Horn* (c.1170) and *Brut* (c.1155), the verbs *chanter* and *organer* appear to relate to singing, perhaps solo melody and some kind of ensemble[18] respectively. *Brut* also refers to organs:

quant la messe fu comenciee	when the mass was begun,
ke le jur fu mult exalciee	which was very exultant on that day,
mult oïssiez orgues suner	you could hear the organs playing loudly,
e clers chanter e organer.	clerics chanting and singing in ensemble.

The Breton cycle *Lancelot* (c.1170) specifies occasion, context and the presence of the *plebes*: at Whit or on Christmas Day (? – *a Pentecoste ou a Noel*) the people go to the monastery (*mostier*) to hear the organ (Perrot 1965: 299). Such texts picture the ideal scene in a major Norman monastery, and by this date *organa* in church is likely to mean 'organ' in such poems. Easter too became a time suitable for organ-sound, one of the regular feasts for which organs were specified in later service-plans and contracts. An early recorded example is St Peter, Erfurt, in 1226, when the new organ, a 'wonderful piece of work', was first heard over the Easter weekend *(in sabatho sancto pasche . . . mirificium opus* – MGH SS 30.1.390).

Many details are unclear in Gervase of Canterbury's report of Canterbury Cathedral a few years after its fire of 1174.[19] In the Norman cathedral, both nave *(aula)* and quire had special equipment made of worked metal (a large gilt crown-candelabrum), while the south transept also had an organ on the upper of two floors, near the altar to All Saints in the eastern

[18] i.e. several voices singing much the same melody in different versions at the same time, as distinct from polyphony (different melodies or lines at the same time).
[19] In Willis: 34–47 and Davis-Weyer: 141–6.

apse of that transept. How old the organ was is not clear from
Gervase's account, but he probably means it was made before
1174. Perhaps the bellows were below, on the ground floor?
Positioned some way from the monastic choir east of the crossing
tower, it cannot have formed an intimate part in the liturgy. But it
was close to pilgrim-processions moving down to the crypt on the
south side (where the altars included St Augustine of Canterbury's) and across to the place of martyrdom of St Thomas Becket
(†1170) in the north transept. Perhaps the organ was built for
playing to pilgrims as they passed along to the crypt or transepts.

Other details about organs emerge from brief English
references at this period. An organ at Abingdon – a more
recent instrument than that made in the tenth century, which
had been carted off by the Vikings meanwhile – was endowed
by the donor for repairs and maintenance.[20] Such abbeys may
have had a succession of organs, replaced as they became
unusable or outmoded, and associated with special festive
events like the reception of new abbots, as at Bury St
Edmunds in 1182. At Rochester in 1192 there is information
on both the giving and placing of the organ: a stone cloister
(complete with south quire aisle – Johnson: 2) and an organ
were given by the Norman bishop, and they were probably
situated close together on the south side of the church. Other
references, however, may still use *organum* in an old sense, as at
Winchester in 1172 when the bishop made over monies for 'the
making of books and the repairing of organs' according to the
translation (Goodman: 3), or at Ely in 1133 when the bishop
gave some tithes 'for the maintenance of *organa*' and 'for making and repairing the books of the church'.[21] On both occasions,
organa very likely meant psalters or some kind of chant-book.

Examples from the Thirteenth Century

The increasing detail in references of the thirteenth century
is by no means always much clearer. The costs specified in the
Fabric Rolls at Exeter in 1286/7 'concerning the enclosing of
the organ'[22] could refer either to some wooden casework or

[20] Reports of the Vikings at Abingdon in RBMAS 2.2.278 (they came up the
Thames?) and of the maintenance endowment in 2.2.208.
[21] *Ad emendationem organorum* and *ad libros ecclesiae faciendos et emendandos*: Stubbs: xxvi.
[22] *In expensis circa organa claudenda . . . 4s*: in Erskine: 7. This is the first known
reference to organs at Exeter.

(more likely) to some new locks on access doors. The implications of a chronicle entry at Strasbourg in 1292 are that the minster's organ was a major instrument (MGH SS 17.103, 139), but nothing is said on whether this was a 'swallownest' organ – a large timber structure like those hanging on the upper nave-wall of many a fourteenth- and fifteenth-century cathedral.

In fact, where an organ was placed is generally quite unclear in the documentation. Presumably the clerks or chroniclers referring to an instrument knew where it was, but since the very earliest organs were likely not to have been fixed, it is a pity that there is too little evidence for one to trace what had happened over the centuries. A clue for more than one later church might be found in the list of items burned in a fire, as at St Maria zu den Staffeln, Mainz, in 1285 where it seems that the organ was near an altar (Bösken: 90), but it is often impossible to infer much. Yet although so little is certain about the structure and location of thirteenth-century organs, the fact that a newly built organ gets referred to in the chronicles – as distinct from the account-books – at least suggests that it was a large, fixed instrument attracting interest.

The phrase 'new organ' *(organa nova)* is not uncommon in the thirteenth century, and many important churches are likely to have had an organ at each of the stages of their constant reconstruction and gothic modernizing. Large-scale timber-work for gorgeous galleries and casework, polished pewter for larger and larger front pipes: these would amount to a conspicuous 'new organ', a dazzling object to appeal to the people. In the thirteenth-century chronicle recording the organ of Prague Cathedral (Sv. Víta), there are only a handful of items for the year 1255 but they include both the cost and schedule for the *organa nova* (FRB 2.293). Such references are quite typical of the vast stretch of country from the Rhine to the Elbe, not least the Rhineland itself (Strasbourg, Worms, Mainz, Koblenz, Bonn).

Clearly, the mid-thirteenth century did see new directions in organ-building, especially in central and east-central Europe. There seems suddenly to have been many new organs, probably all-encased instruments larger than before, aiming for a bigger or less localized sound in the new and very large churches; sometimes they replaced earlier organs; often they must have taken some time to build and to set up; and usually by now they were often being made by contracted, named craftsmen. In these various later sources two particular words are sometimes misleading: the old term *organista* and the new term 'larger organs'.

If in many a late twelfth-century cathedral *organista* meant a director of the choral music or organum, as it did at Tarragona in 1164, perhaps it did gradually come more and more to mean 'organist' in the thirteenth century, especially in Spain. But the word itself is hardly evidence that these churches had an organ, or if they did, that the *organista* actually played them, much less that they were played as often as polyphony was sung. Farther afield older terminology may have persisted longer: the *organista seu cantor* at Olomouc Cathedral in 1257 or the *magister organorum* for the Dominican sisters of St Margaret's Isle, Budapest, in 1303, are even less likely to have been actual organists.[23]

In the case of the term 'larger organs', annals at Durham in 1264 report construction of a *magnum campanile* and *organa grandiora* when no smaller organ is known about (Raine: 46). Assuming that *organa* does not mean merely some ingenious *machine* for the bells or *grandiora* an organ as distinct from smaller musical instruments, the implication is that there were two organs, a larger for feastday clamour and a smaller for the Office. This was certainly the case at Durham in the sixteenth century, but like any other custom, it had to be established. It seems unlikely that even a major cathedral or abbey had both a large and a small fixed organ before *c.*1350, and any apparent references to such a pair earlier could well be misleading. But here and there it cannot be quite out of the question, when either one of the organs – the smaller for playing in the quire, the larger for entertaining the *plebes* – could have been the more recent.

With the later thirteenth century an array of further technical or practical detail appears in references, culminating in the formal contract. Much of the earliest surviving contractual documentation of any kind in England – orders for building work of various kinds – comes from royal order-books which, though not itemized contracts themselves, suggest the sort of bookkeeping that would lead cathedrals to want contracts to be drawn up as this particular piece of expensive equipment

[23] Details of Spanish cathedrals in Anglés: 564, 848. Olomouc in Senhal: 37. Budapest in Zolnay: 399. These three authors assume that *organista* implies the presence of an organ.

became common. An early organ contract is that of 1259 at Barcelona Cathedral (contract both for building and for maintenance), while at Wells Cathedral in 1310 the Chapter Minutes, themselves new sources of such information, provide for the felling of trees and taking of timber for the construction of organs and presumably their gallery.[24]

Part of the purpose of contracts is to specify materials, presumably because they have to be bought in against eventual repayment, and such details increase during the fourteenth century. Materials at the Chapter's charge include lead at York Minster in 1338, and 'good, fine and dry wood' with 'good boards and good deerskin' for the bellows at Barcelona in 1345.[25] At Barcelona, the keys were to be of boxwood and holly, presumably either for differentiated naturals and sharps or for inlaid decoration. Fourteenth-century Italian contracts often mention tools[26] for an organ-workshop that had to be set up locally, no doubt often in the church itself. By 1379, the contract at SS. Annunziata, Florence has reached the stage of unrivalled importance for an understanding of current organ-building (see Taucci). Details include the tuning system, pedal mechanism, chest, keys and compass, pipes (hammered and polished tin), bellows of calfskin, a carved and painted case (with a cover of some kind, made of cloth stretched over a frame), and even a monochord soundboard[27] inside the organ to give the pitches for tuning the pipes: a brilliant idea.

With this contract, the history of organs has reached a point after which virtually every aspect of their development can be documented – not for a further century in great detail, perhaps, but increasingly so as the civilization that developed organs came also to rely on written, technical description. Organists themselves seldom appreciate the part played by their instrument in the West's move towards careful documentation.

[24] Barcelona in Llovera: 174. Wells in Bird: 1.154.
[25] York in Freeman, Barcelona in Baldelló: 199.
[26] Iron mandrel (S. Maria, Gemona, 1373), soldering irons (Siena Cathedral, 1372), and casting benches (ditto), as well as musical details (thirteen sharps or *semitoniis* at Treviso in 1347), quoted in Donati: 152, 153, 201 and 233.
[27] A slim, hollow box with a single string stretched along it on bridges, one of which is movable to give finely differentiated pitches.

4

What Did
Early Organs Do?

Processions and Other Events

The Mediterranean climate must have made the organ useful out of doors in both pagan and early Christian com-
munities, and some suggestions have been made in earlier
chapters about events at which its sound would have been
heard. Most if not all of these events were public, often
rowdy, without the quiet intimacy of sound associated with
some much later organ-music.

Although references rarely even hint at what exactly is
being played, an interesting clue is given in several accounts
from Constantinople in the ninth and tenth centuries
(Schuberth: 68ff, 82). They say that at a palace reception or
when 'Holy! Holy! Holy!' is sung out of doors, the signal for
continuing the proceedings is given *by the organ-sound ceasing*.
Silence as organs and bells fall silent is not infrequently mentioned as a cue for something to happen, as at Bury St
Edmunds in 1182 when the prior began prayers in the recep-
tion-service for the new abbot, according to a rare but surely
typical report (RBMAS 96.1.230–1). What needs to be
envisioned here is not today's quiet organ-prelude before a
service begins – soft, low-pitched music dying away as the
priest enters – but a noisy, continuous, sustained sound
rather like a siren's, as loud and high-pitched as bells, the
kind of sound originally associated with outdoor events. Sudden silence would be very striking.

The shouts of 'Holy!' as the emperor was acclaimed at certain ceremonies in Constantinople were imitated to some
extent at the Carolingian court. It is significant that the
Frankish king Pippin was sent his Byzantine organ of 757
soon after being anointed in St-Denis (see p. 33), for a custom
with newly crowned emperors in Constantinople was that

they were publicly acclaimed in the great church of Hagia Sophia. Is this why the emperor sent Pippin an *organum* – it was thought appropriate that he should be acclaimed too? Shouts of praise *(laudes)* are similar to the cries of *Sanctus* that had become part of the mass, and even if a tenth-century Benedictine cantor knew nothing of practices either at Constantinople or at Charlemagne's court, he could have read of similar practices in David and Solomon's Temple:

organis et aliis musicis	praise sounded aloud by organs and
instrumentis concrepari,	other musical instruments,
et a populo laudes	and was shouted out by the people,
conclamari,	
(PL 172.556)	

in the words of a twelfth-century commentator. Where organs were beginning to get known, knowledge of such Old Testament practice would justify their presence or perhaps encourage a monastery to commission a new one. Even the last quotation's reference to the people *(populus, plebes)* gives an indispensable detail to the picture of how organs were getting known: they were there for the sake of public ceremony or public splendour – the public whose participation was being periodically championed (ideally at least) by reform-minded bishops.

Various particular opportunities for the sound of *organa* – at the acclamations for a ruler, at the dedications of a new monastery – are associated with processions in so far as most major Mediterranean events would involve outdoor processing in one form or another. It is difficult now to appreciate the significance to a community, before and after Christianity became acceptable, of processing from one place to another for so many of its communal acts. (The gospels themselves describe several important processions, including the *adventus* on Palm Sunday and the walk of the condemned to Calvary.) But even during short processions within such services as baptism, or while the *Thrice Holy!* was sung before lessons, some music could have filled the gap, as it did and still does for the gradual of the mass.

At the grand dedication by the pope at Cava in 1092 (see p. 61), the instruments are mentioned immediately after the pope is reported as 'delineating the walls' and completing the circuit of space to be consecrated. This ceremony was distinct from both mass and office, but one can assume that at other times festive mass was itself the occasion for the processing, the special vestments, the special effects of light or sound, and so on. In the Benedictine north, it is difficult to believe that the 1,250 lamps used at St-Denis on feastdays, according to a description of 799 (in Bischoff), were not matched by brilliant music, equally *artificial* in making use of some man-made apparatus, in this case instruments.

To the organ-historian, quite the most evocative of all descriptions of a church event in the years around *c.*1000 is that concerning the dedication of the fenland monastery-church at Ramsey on 8 November 991, written by the author of the *Life of St Oswald* a few years later (before 1005). Given the unexceptional nature of this abbey, already remarked on in chapter 3, one can take this description as typical of many that could have been made at the time, descriptions of church dedications, bishop's consecrations, royal acclamations, translations of relics and other communal events:

introeuntibus praesulibus et ducibus, abbatibus et militibus, populus est aggregatus immensus . . .	the bishops, nobles, abbots and knights having entered, a large crowd of people congregated . . .
Explicito sollemni jubilo responsorio, laus laudibus hymnisque hymnus allectus est. Namque magister organorum cum agmine ascendit populorum in altis sedibus, quo tonitruali sonitu excitavit mentes fidelium laudare nomen Domini.	When the solemn, jubilant responsory was completed, praise upon praise and hymn upon hymn were sung in sequence [?]. Whereupon the master of the *organa* ascended with the crowd of people to the upper floor, where with thundering sound he stirred up the souls of the faithful to praise the name of the Lord.
Haec audiens gratulans chorus auribus benignis, Christo, sanctorum qui est decus Angelorum studuerunt melos psallere,	The joyful choir, hearing this with kindly ears, for Christ, who is the glory of the holy angels, applied themselves to psalmody,

dulces alternatim	singing sweet praises lustily
concrepando laudes. Cum	in alternation. When the
dextera pars	right-hand part [of the choir]
sonum melodum personaret	sang out the melody with
inclytis vocibus,	glorious voices,
tum sinister jubilando	then the left jubilantly
organicis desudabat	exerted themselves in *organic*
laudibus.	praises.
(RBMAS 71.1.464–5)	

There seems to be a further reference to an Anglo-Saxon dedication, at Winchester; see p. 78. If the Ramsey description means that music was performed antiphonally between organ and chorus, then any organ at Ramsey would have had to be thoroughly modern and able to play agile melody.

Perhaps it was and did, but both *organorum* and *organicis* would then have to denote 'the organ', which would be unusual in such reports even though Ramsey is known to have had an organ (see p. 6). If on the other hand *organorum* and *organicis* refer to ensemble music for voices contrasting with the chanted psalms, what followed the sound of the organ might have been ensemble music for voices. This is a point of some significance, because the Ramsey report is the fullest indication of what organs and choirs were doing by *c.*1000. The question it raises is: Was the organ still producing only 'sounds', or was it playing 'music'? Was the keyboard's potential to produce 'well-modulated melody' already so developed that it could make a partnership with a choir singing polyphony of some kind? It is not possible to say with certainty, although most interpretations, affected by knowledge of later music, have assumed the latter.

Whatever the truth, the Ramsey report does give an evocative picture. As the monks and nobles enter a new church for an exceptional event of thanksgiving, a large crowd gathers, the monks begin to sing the office of vespers, a procession takes the crowds to a gallery where they are then inspired by the organ, and various *organal* music follows. This is a scene that could have been repeated in hundreds of new abbeys from the English Fenlands to the deep valleys of the Alps, from the foothills of the Spanish Pyrenees to those of the Harz mountains. The only difference was that the farther south the ceremony, the more parts of it are likely to have taken place out of doors.

The Origins of 'Organ Music'?

It must have been very rare before the fifteeenth century for either secular cathedrals or monasteries to make use of organs for the daily office or for the mass itself except on a dozen or so feastdays. To imagine quite how they were used, then, is a matter of speculating on what they might have done on festive occasions and what uses they could have had outside services.

Neither is documented fully or clearly, especially the use of organs outside services. It has to remain a guess, but a plausible one, that organs supplied background sounds while pilgrims visited shrines or when people gathered for other reasons, as was common enough in medieval churches and in some of those that changed allegiance in Protestant times. The more regular these assemblies had become, the easier it is to understand how the tradition arose in the later fifteenth century for public organ recitals in some of the larger town churches of the Netherlands: perhaps organs had long played while merchants gathered at midday in the nave of such non-monastic churches, using it as a kind of Exchange.[1]

Part of the many disagreements between bishops and abbots in the twelfth century centred on the use to which the main monastery church was put: the bishop said public masses, but it was not fit for laymen to penetrate the convent.[2] Since organs were there to increase the festiveness, one can surmise that they were not involved in the monks' own regular services. Positioned near public entrances or in circulation spaces, their sound would not have been intimate enough for the quire, and it is much more likely that when organs did eventually come to participate more in the regular mass and office, they were made to modest dimensions within the quire space itself.

Usually, this might mean their being placed, whatever

[1] If the local church nave had the only reasonably reliable clock accessible to the public, as must usually have been the case, there might have been even more reason to meet there.

[2] e.g. the papal bull of 1146 protecting Peterborough, in Mellows: 114.

their shape, above the stalls: under an arch on the north side (the main arcade, or a specially made opening) or on the screen at the west side (positioned on the north end of it?). Many centuries later the organ in the gothic cathedral of Winchester, placed above the stalls on the north side, had a wooden wall behind and above it, somewhat like a tester directing the sound down to the singers in the quire. One wonders how old this idea was. Presumably, placing and structuring in any such way must have depended on how developed wooden stalls themselves were, and these were rarely planned in regular form or on a large scale much before the beginning of the thirteenth century. No doubt it would not take too many years before a major church had both a 'public' and a 'conventual' organ, a large nave instrument and a smaller one in the quire. By 1500 this was virtually a standard arrangement.

For the earlier period, a report on the consecration of the rebuilt minster and enclosure at Saxon Winchester in *c.*944 describes the clamour of bells and voices, the jubilation of clergy and public *(plebes)*, and the special music added to the regular liturgical chant for such a festive occasion. The details occur in lines 239–42 of Wulfstan's poem quoted further in chapter 5:

> *cimbalicae voces calamis miscentur acutis*
> bell-like voices [of boys?] are mingled with high pipes [= organ?]
> *disparibusque tropis dulce camena sonat,*
> and melody sweetly sounds in very varied kinds of trope,
> *insuper et cleri iubilat plebs omnis, et infans.*
> and above, the clergy, the boys and all the common people rejoice.
> (Campbell: 72)

Whether 'varied kinds of trope' meant newly composed music – as distinct both from chant and from ensemble singing as it could have been traditionally improvised – is not known. Nevertheless, one can imagine that cantors of major abbeys in about 1000 were moving more towards composed and notated music, music essentially different from the kind of counterpoint many cultures have been able to sing and play without notation.

New kinds of composed pieces not only sowed the seeds for

future developments in music but could have been accompanied by another trend: Western monasteries were becoming interested in instrument-technology. Already in the ninth century, the newly composed tropes and sequences associated with the monk Tuotilo of St Gall were said to have been conceived 'by means of the psaltery or rote'[3] (MGH SS 2.101), and while an organ is not mentioned in this connection, one can imagine that both new musical compositions and experiments with instruments of various kinds do somehow go together, or would do so in the better-equipped monasteries. Once the notion exists that someone has a special skill in something (as Tuotilo was said to have in instrument-playing), development becomes inevitable.

A possible clue as to what happened in some services is given by a book written at Winchester in about 1000, in which some of the new pieces were written down with the addition of a few note-letters above the plainsong:[4]

Example 3

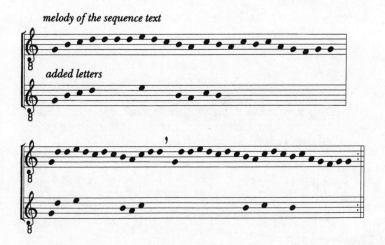

melody of the sequence text

added letters

---

[3] i.e. string instruments, plucked or bowed.
[4] Verses 14/15 and 22/23 of the 24-verse sequence *Cithara:* transcription and notes in Holschneider 1978: 166.

Whether or not these letters are actual notes intended for the organist to play at the same time, the new sequences and festive tropes both at Winchester and St Gall (and the many less prominent monasteries in their sphere of influence) could well have had *organa* contributing something of this kind, picking out some of the sung notes. One cannot always be sure why precisely these notes were written in and not others, but in this sequence the letters always stop some time before those of the voice. It is tempting to see here the organ making use of its sustained notes.

Organa also eventually contributed to one particular form of feastday music: the Sepulchre Play and other 'plays', in which a scene appropriate to the day was enacted in church, with the sound of bells and (sooner or later) organs participating in the action or rounding it off during the final singing of a *Te deum*. This was a hymn in which such clamour traditionally played a part. In fact, the *Te deum* may have played a crucial part in organs becoming known to Western Christendom. Bells and the *Te deum* are documented in the West well before 1000, and the idea of festive clamour could easily take in the organ, either in addition to bells or instead of them. Moreover the organ keyboard could pick out certain notes from the repetitious *Te deum* chant to make something of a motif for itself:

Example 4

v1   *Te De-um lau- da- mus: te Do- mi- num con-fi- te- mur.*

v2   *Te ae-ter- num Pa- trem om-nis ter- ra ve-ne- ra- mur.*

organ motif:

In introducing its motif from time to time throughout the chant, the organ would add to the jubilation naturally associated with this text and the special occasions on which it was sung. The somewhat repetitive nature of the chant could also lead the organist to want to hold a long drone (E?) like the bagpipes. The jangle of some bells playing the same notes in a *Te deum* would also create a kind of note-cluster, and the organ could easily add multiple drones to it.

Dante's remarks on *organi* and the *Te deum* (*Purgatorio* IX.139–45, early fourteenth century) are a late reference to two things traditionally associated with each other, although, as is often the case, what precisely the poet is describing is not as certain as first appears. He is speaking of the *Te deum* being sung while other noises were heard, the whole giving him a familiar impression, as

> *quando a cantar con organi si stea;*
> when one stands to sing with the organ;
> *ch'or sì, or no s'intendon le parole.*
> that now one hears the words, now one does not.

This need not mean that the organ and voices were alternating systematically verse by verse, but – something that would be older and less sophisticated – that the organ played its motif from time to time, loudly enough to cover the words being sung at that moment. At St Albans in 1235 a situation of comparable clamour is described: as the abbot-elect was led into the church and then processed to the high altar, the *Te deum* was begun, bells, the organ *(burdones)* and the clock all sounded, and candles around the altar were lit (RBMAS 28.5.520). The picture is of a special occasion with special personages present, a procession with a formal liturgy of some kind, and a singing of the *Te deum*, with bells, instruments, sources of light and clamour. Everything about it is jubilant, the kind of event which was common over several centuries and familiar in hundreds of monasteries across Europe.

Now if one were to make a guess how the organ progressed from supplying *festive noises* to *true organ music*, one would first have to avoid any anachronistic distinction between 'noise' and 'music'. Rather, it was that the nature of the sounds which were contributed by the organ gradually

changed. Festive noises were indeed organ music in any
tenth-century definition of such word, for the organ did what
no other single instrument could do: sustain at a high volume-
level a tone which was in tune with others, i.e. each calculated
according to the proportions.[5] 'Noises' would become 'music'
as the succession of notes imitated actual melodies and moved
with greater agility over a bigger compass. The following
might offer some pointers as to how such changes gradually
came about. As to why they came about: one can only suppose
that organ-sounds were as restlessly developed as various
other elements that supported the central, unchanging acts of
devotion in church.

At first, in one or two major churches here and there, an
organ contributed some sustained notes and added to the
clamour at certain events, especially if it were placed in a public part of the church. This would be part of the traditional
contribution organs made to many kinds of ceremony, the
kind of sound expected from it. The sustained note could be a
drone in the treble, tenor or bass, or it could be combined with
other notes in a familiar chord (a fifth, a triad), and it would be
rather siren-like. Perhaps in some appropriate chant such as
the *Te deum*, the keyboard could do more than hold a note or
two and would repeat a phrase of melody, adding to the jubilant effect.

By nature such a phrase, sung or played, contains the basic
notes of the scale, which are also those of the most familiar
chords. How or when chords were made on a keyboard can
only be guessed – it was surely a question first of holding down
a single drone – but in any case one should not underestimate
the melodious effect of playing simple phrases made
up from the notes C D E F G A.[6] Perhaps the organ sometimes
continued to repeat a melodic phrase, sustaining the notes
and creating a kind of cluster effect, not unlike bells but of
course not percussive, its sound more sweetly and evenly

[5] Vocal counterpoint sung to the same rationally derived notes, those of the 'white
note scale', would be equally *organic*.
[6] That is, the hexachord. One can occasionally hear pure hexachordal sounds
in much later music, as at the close of two of Chopin's Nocturnes (last five
bars of Op. 15 no. 2 in F sharp major and last two bars of Op. 9 no. 3 in B
major).

sustained.[7] Perhaps in time it began to anticipate the melody of a newly composed piece of music (such as a trope or sequence), eventually alternating with the voices in a regular way.

Then, as this became customary, or as the organ was more frequently placed near the quire, it also contributed some such music, intermittently or in alternation, to the *Introit* or *Sanctus*. The custom must then have arisen for playing the same kind of music in the canticles and psalms of the office, partly no doubt because of the length of the psalms, and one can assume that strictly alternating the choir and the organ came about only after organs had for some time been playing more freely and intermittently. What the organ eventually played amounted to a verse of the psalm: a musical phrase of decent length, during which the choir of monks was silent, speaking inwardly the unsung verses before and after those they were to sing aloud. At this point in its evolution, the organ's music would surely be more regular in metre, with shaped melodic periods, its texture moving towards the 'organ counterpoint' of the Renaissance and thus towards more recent ideas on what constitutes true organ music.

Organs and Organum

Some guesses on how organs and music are connected at a deeper level have been made in chapter 1. Here the focus is more on what organs might have been brought in to do when they were first getting known in the monastic churches of northwestern Europe.

The idea that the organ provided an accompaniment to the chant and that ensemble music for non-unison voices was called '*organum*' because it sounded like an organ, was plausible only so long as the many meanings of the word *organum* were not systematically traced. Of course, it is always possible that somewhere in *c*.1000 an organ did play in vocal music or

---

[7] Some later canons – 'Frère Jacques', for example – create a sound-cluster not unlike the bells mentioned in the text, if they are sung repetitively and continuously so as to produce (in C major) the notes G c d e f g a all at once. This cluster is both triadic (G c e g) and hexachordal (c d e f g a), as some early organ-sounds would also have been.

did inspire some choirs of monks to imitate the things its keyboard could do, such as produce a melody on several levels at once ('parallels'), hold a note below or above the chant ('drone'), play the chant itself ('*cantus firmus*') while others sang around it ('heterophony' or 'polyphony'),[8] and so on. But there is no clear evidence that it did, and too many practical and rather mundane questions would have to be answered – what kind of keyboard did it have, was the organ located near the singers, was its wind-raising reliable enough? – before idle speculation could become anything else.

In the Carolingian period, *organum* was organized ensemble music, a music distinct from two other kinds of sound produced by groups of people: the disorganized crowd noises at acclamations, and the concordant choir music of voices singing in unison for the monastic psalms. A theorist like Regino of Prüm (*c*.900) would use the phrase *in organo* to mean 'in music of more than one sound', that is to say 'in organized music'.[9] The term itself could embrace instruments if any were available, but that must have been seldom – at most, special occasions in special churches. How this early *organized music* was organized, whether it was planned or entirely improvised, must have varied. But musical techniques that were basic, traditional and universal – such as drones, parallels and heterophony – would have needed little planning or directing.

In this connection, St Augustine's commentary on Psalm 150 is again especially useful since it gave countless later readers in the West the idea that ensemble sounds could and would join together in praise, which was all the justification musical clergy needed:

non ut singulae sonent, sed ut diversitate concordissima consonent sicut ordinatur in organo.	so that they sound not singly but together in the most harmonious diversity, as is ordered in *organum*.

[8] Heterophony: playing or singing decoratively around the notes of a melody being sung or played at the same time. (Example 3 shows the organ moving more slowly than the voices.) The result is a kind of polyphony.
[9] Again, 'organized' would mean notes specifically produced by a proportional or 'organic' scale of tuned notes, as distinct from random sounds or those not in a tuned scale.

Habebunt enim etiam sancti	For the saints too will differ
differentiam ad suos	harmoniously, not
consonantes, non	disharmoniously, from their
dissonantes.	fellows.
(PL 37.1964)	

The psalmist's line 'Praise him on the strings and pipe' *(in chordis et organo)* therefore indicates something more than single sounds of praise: *organum* is a music that is neither unison nor solo but ensemble, expressing unity in diversity, the idea being of differences which work together, whether vocal, instrumental or both. *'Organum'* may not *mean* organ or imply some kind of organ-like sound, but it does not exclude either of them from what it does broadly signify, namely, ensemble praise in music: many separate elements working towards one common cause, a metaphor for the Church itself.

If, as well he might by the early eleventh century, a theorist thinks that *organum* is correctly used only to denote vocal counterpoint or polyphony (e.g. Sachs 1980: 234), perhaps it was because he was far more familiar with such music than with the sounds of an actual organ. Sometimes for theorists the term is even more specific: it denotes vocal music that makes use only of the basic *organic* intervals of the octave, fifth and fourth, not the more free-for-all array of intervals sung in other and earlier kinds of music, such as certain folk-music from which the Church's music was now to be quite distinct. In any case, for centuries it must have been more important for books to give an account of vocal music than to describe organs made with pipes and bellows.

By *c.*1100, one Johannes, an influential south German writer known as Affligemensis, thought vocal *organum* so called because

similitudinem exprimat	it expresses a similarity
instrumenti quod organum	with the instrument that is
vocatur.	called organ.
(CSM 1.157)	

John may be merely suggesting that voices joining together in ensemble music are like organs playing more than one pipe per key, as indeed they are. One cannot make from it a description of 'music sounding in parallel fifths' or 'melismatic melodies sung or played in certain conventionalized rhythmic patterns over long-held notes of the chant', of the kind that would have been heard by 1200 in a few major cathedrals of northwest Europe.[10] Using the word *organum* only to mean such full-dress polyphony notated for voices, as most musical dictionaries still do, can mislead one from its older and simpler meaning of 'organized ensemble music'.

Since so little is known about both how ensemble music was sung in *c.*1000 and what organs were capable of, one has to conjecture from the very possibility that Example 3 (see p. 79) shows the kind of music an organ could play while festive chant was being sung. More still might be conjectured by considering that, in principle, the keyboard of an organ can play in any of the following ways:

if it has seven or eight notes	*if it has fifteen notes*
— antiphony (i.e. playing a chant in alternation with the choir)	— antiphonal response up or down an octave
— parallels (playing the chant in fourths or fifths)	— parallels (now also in octaves, perhaps some twelfths?)
— heterophony	— heterophony at the octave above
— canon	— canon at the octave above or below
— drones	— drones (doubled or tripled)
— a held chord	— more held chords
— ostinato (repeated phrase, as in the *Te deum*)	— ostinato
— combinations of these	— more combinations of these

Of course, the effects could be varied: the ostinato need not be continuous, canon could alternate with passages above a drone, and so on. Clearly, the longer the organ's compass the more techniques are possible, and one wonders whether players anticipating musical possibilities prompted builders

[10] Parallel fifths: the same melody sung at two pitches, a fifth apart. Melismatic: freer melodies, sung to one syllable or a few syllables, often semi-improvised by a soloist.

to increase the compass or whether builders learning to handle a wider range of pipe-lengths prompted players to expand their music. My own guess would be the latter rather than the former, that European builders, whoever they were, were less conformist than cantors (see also below, p. 134). Builders could have been more inventive than the chant-singers on one hand and the old Roman makers of water-organs on the other, less tied by the conventions of their community, monastic or commercial, than either of these were.

And yet, not a single one of the musical techniques listed is described in the references to organs. Even the drone, which is the simplest of them, is barely documented for organs before the thirteenth century, and then only in reference to or in drawings of *bourdons* (Sachs 1980: 348), behind which word there is a complicated etymology that is not very informative about what organs actually played. But it is not difficult to believe that any form of organ-keyboard, however early, would have led to various experiments in sound on at least the rowdier feastdays. Even a simple keyboard would make possible not only melodies (in unison, at the octave, or more freely para phrased) but certain basic ways of making counterpoint, such as:

note-against-note music, perhaps favouring now parallels, now contrary motion;

drones added to a single-line melody – short or long, fixed or moving, from one stretch of melody to another;

an independent contribution such as ostinato;

sustained chords: including, perhaps, the basic notes played together to give an effect not unlike the clangour of bells.

The last is even less documented than the others but is not out of the question: like sirens, perhaps like Roman or Byzantine organs, the Western Christian organs could have played note-clusters or chords of one kind or another, screeching across the open spaces of a *monasterium* (enclo-sure), summoning the *plebes*, and adding to the noise on cer-tain occasions in or out of church. Hence the remark in the Winchester poem (line 164 – see p. 115) that the organ was so loud that no other sound could be heard through it. Assum-ing this is more than a traditional reference to the loudness of organs – it is certainly that – maybe the organ was meant to be penetrating, playing not a lively piece of Gregorian chant but sounds more like those of a siren. The same could be said of the same poem's *thundering* images: however conventional these might be, thunderousness would be increased the more notes were being played at once.

The twenty or even forty keys that the Winchester organ was said to have were more than any chants would have needed, even when performed *organally*, and its phalanx of bellows could surely have allowed chords to be sustained as long as desired. Perhaps that is why so many bellows were needed on the bigger occasions. Also, if its keys were sliders, pushed in and pulled out and not returning automatically through a spring, then playing a drone or several drones was easy. In this respect, a 'more advanced' keyboard made up of pressed keys which return to position was less convenient: to make a held note on such keyboards, one has to keep it down by hand (see also the remarks on p. 129). Perhaps Roman circus-organs also had sliders that did not automatically return to position, something not incompatible with the extant representations, such as they are.

However like a siren an organ in *c*.1000 was, or however simple its music, whether playing alone or with singers, the experience in sound it offered was startling. Its fixed notes, their tuning, the timbre of its bronze pipes, the complexity of each note (more than one pipe), the fact that it was sustained: all this was a new world of sound and would surely be developed, given the circumstances surrounding early organs in western Europe. For not only were groups of creative men embellishing the liturgy and composing new music, they were also finding ways to record it in new notations. At the same time they were exploring other developments in the mechanical and technical arts for the greater glory of God, including the building of totally new kinds of church-space in which everything – technology, architecture, liturgy, music – was fresh, novel, inventive, based on earlier achievements but not held back by them.

Where Were Organs Put?

In the courtyard of a Mediterranean church-complex or in

the open porch of a northern abbey (such as can still be seen at Fleury), the sound of an organ placed there would certainly travel and was meant to do so. If organs came into church with processions of one kind or another, entering through public doors at the west end, they might be temporarily placed there or kept for the next procession. The more permanent their location, the more they could grow. And the bigger the apparatus for raising wind (a larger number of bellows, a more extensive framework to hold them), the more the organ needed to be fixed in a rigid structure, even if it remained movable.

Another possibility was that organs, donated as valuable objects, could be placed near the altar of a particular saint, as seems to have been the case at Winchester and Malmesbury. Since all of the major and even quite minor monastic churches held sacred relics viewed by the populace, these altars too were public, and instruments would be used when the people were there for festive processions or for other moments on certain 'Sundays and Feastdays', as many a reference puts it. Such special objects, perhaps with cumbersome bellows, were less portable than traditional *organa*, and would justify their presence there as Christian temple-furniture by means of the authority they drew from St Augustine.

Such a picture is not easy to establish step by step. In most cases where a great deal is known about the plan of a church associated with an early organ (Winchester, Cava, Abingdon, Ramsey, Fécamp, Bruges, Lobbes, Petershausen), or in monasteries where organ-writings originated (Helmarshausen, Cologne St Pantaleon, Rheims, St Gall, Murbach, Freising, Hirsau), various sites for the instrument are possible, even when documentation pins it down as narrowly as it does at Canterbury or Bruges. Like any period, the years in which such monasteries contributed to the theory or practice of making organs also saw the rebuilding of their church, even its massive reconstruction, part of which may well have been for the sake of an organ. At Hirsau during the abbacy of William (†1091), whose writings on the proportional measurements of organ-pipes suggest a certain practical knowledge, the church was rebuilt to a large three-aisle basilica with a two-storey westwork, all giving several possible sites for an organ which, however, is never mentioned in the abbey's documents.

By the year 1000 or so, in all of these cases, from Wessex to Lake Constance, the building had some form of complex western structure: facing east, perhaps with only modest openings to the nave, there was an upper-floor space with an altar, or a multi-storeyed westwork, even a whole west-church which itself had two spacious floors. Westworks were particularly useful for processions and pilgrim-tours, giving churches in northern Europe the kind of processional spaces that had been provided by the courtyards or the outdoor pro-cessional routes of southern complexes. They gave a sense of occasion each time one entered the more open and lighter nave from them. They may also have provided suitable spaces for liturgical drama or its processions, and the possi-bility that organs somehow contributed to such events by the eleventh century or early twelfth exists in the case of a whole series of major abbeys: Winchester, Fleury, St-Riquier, Gorze, Metz, Laon, Soissons, Toul, Verdun, Limoges St-Martial, St Gall, the Reichenau, Augsburg, Minden and (above all) Cluny.

Some churches had a gallery elsewhere in the building and nearer the main altar or crypt, perhaps a two-storeyed bay or porch *(porticus)* whose upper floor gave a good site for an organ. But since over the whole period before the twelfth century it cannot be shown that the organ directly served the office or regular mass, a likelier location than quire or cros-sing was one of the more public, less conventual areas of the building, such as a westwork or a pavement-level space away from the choir. A location favoured in the late Middle Ages – the 'swallownest' perched on the nave wall somewhere above the main arcade – (see above, p. 70) – could be a late instance of siting organs chiefly in order to appeal to the *plebes*, to give them something to stand below and admire. But even with swallownests, the uniqueness of each of the major churches of Europe meant individual solutions to the question of where the organ was to be placed.

The increasingly frequent reference to organs in the twelfth and thirteenth centuries suggests that they were part of the sudden flowering of timberwork, notably wooden screens and tiered choirstalls with canopies. Much of this had the eventual effect of reducing the amount of walking or processing that had been so regular and frequent in the Church's services. Early organ-structures, each of them individual and even idiosyncratic, gave way to a more common and conventionalized instrument, reflecting the by then conventionalized arrangement of all the church furniture.

Some Influential Locations

Individual buildings associated with early organs serve to suggest what the factors were for placing and making use of them. A characteristic example for the eleventh century in the central Meuse region is Lobbes (*c*.1070–90) where there was no nave gallery but complex east and west ends, rebuilt and added to from time to time, with various suitable sites for an organ away from the pavement. In most monastic houses reformed under the local Brogne-Gorze influence (one of several reform movements of the period), there were three main altars: at the westwork, in the middle of the nave and in the quire above the crypt. An organ would have been suitable near any of them, perhaps audible down in the town if it were placed somewhere in the westwork. Also, the Lobbes church-type must often have had a courtyard, as Brogne did.

A similar need for lengthy processional spaces is at least part of the explanation for the very long naves of English Norman churches begun in the same period as Lobbes, some complete with massive west complexes. Now of course the lengthy processional space is all indoors. It is as if the porch, the enclosed courtyard, narthex and processing aisle were all replaced by one long nave divided by altars or screens and planned for processional 'stations'. For the kinds of need one can imagine arising, an organ could be placed almost anywhere, especially when the choir spread into the nave-bays east of the crossing.

The earlier Anglo-Saxon minster of Winchester never became a familiar type of building but nevertheless remains a useful piece in the puzzle of early organs. Wulfstan's poem describes the organ in that section dealing with the recently completed work in the eastern, not western, part of the church. By *c*.994, the building was some 159′ long, with an aisleless nave, a western structure some 79′ square (larger in area than big German-Saxon churches at Corvey or Werden), a shrine-crypt below the high altar at the eastern 'crossing', an eastern apse and a crypt farther east (above ground, as can still be seen at Werden). Possible locations for the organ at Winchester were:

Towers and western porch. Either might have been open to the outside.

Westwork. A structure east of the western towers, prefacing the nave and probably looking down into it.

North/south porticus (apses). Three successive limbs at the sides of the nave could each have housed an organ, with the bellows at ground level and the chest and keys on the floor above; the first-floor opening need not have been large, or it could have been specially made for the pipe-front (see p. 124). The reference to St Peter in line 172 of the poem would imply that the organ was close to the central altar dedicated to him.

Apses at the 'crossing'. If the organ had a function that was public rather than strictly liturgical, the central space near the main shrine and crypt-steps was a plausible location, for processions no doubt congregated there. The curved bays to the north and south were like 'transepts', built (as the organ probably was) between 980 and 994.

Virtually any place in the church, then, could have served for the organ, reflecting one or other function it had. Archaeological evidence for a bell-casting pit, some feet west of the central space of the crossing,[11] suggests the main bell to have hung in the central tower, and the organ may have been nearby. (An organ in the southern bay would anticipate the later organ-location at Canterbury, even conceivably influencing it.) Curiously, the very choices of interpretation at Winchester anticipate a key question in the history of the organ in Christian Europe: Does it belong to the western or eastern parts of the church?

Any organ there may have been at Aachen nearly two

---

[11] Although a large bell would presumably be cast as directly as possible below where it was to hang, the floor under the tower at Winchester was at the top of some steps, and the casting pit would have had to be dug farther west.

centuries earlier is unlikely to have been fixed in place in the chapel. Nevertheless, the large octagon, complete with a spacious upper floor totally open to the central chapel space, does raise some general questions for the organ-historian. Whenever the emperor received acclamations, standing in the outside tribune looking down into the courtyard or seated on his throne inside looking down on to the altar, a suitable place for a movable Byzantine organ was the gallery, on the west side. This was a space secreted from the *plebes*, but one from which the sound could be heard, both in the courtyard and in the octagon chapel. It would not be a 'church instrument' in any later familiar sense but only in so far as many an imperial ceremony included texts that were liturgical in character, such as cries of 'Holy! Holy! Holy!' Whether any of the bishops visiting Aachen was impressed enough by its practices to wish to exercise his authority at home by imitating them – introducing quasi-regal acclamations with *organa* in his own cathedral, etc. – is not known.

A useful document from the early ninth century is the celebrated and puzzling *Plan of St Gall* (made at Reichenau in c.826/830),[12] a 'schematic guideline' for a monastery, with which many a Benedictine house had details in common. Whatever purpose it had, the Plan's layout clearly expresses some desire for system: compared to the actual layouts of such monasteries as St-Riquier, Hirsau or Bury St Edmunds, it brings everything of the monastery into neat order, including its workshops. The liturgy now appears to be monopolized by the central church, with less emphasis on processional space outside, and once organs became known in such a church they would surely have begun to make a formal liturgical contribution.

The *Plan of St Gall* raises interesting questions about the period, particularly why there are no organs shown on the plan of its church or chapels. Several explanations are possible: it was still too early for a plan to show them; if known at all, organs were too small to be fixed; or they were too exceptional to be shown as necessary furniture like altars and a font, which are marked; or they were seen as ordinary

---

[12] Recent examinations include Sanderson and (connecting the Plan with the abbey church of Reichenau as it was in c.800) Zettler: esp. 14–15, 235–47.

variable equipment like altar-vessels, which are not marked. One could hardly expect a fixed organ to appear on a plan of *c*.830, for it is by no means certain that such a thing yet existed. And yet, since the Plan also makes no mention of bells, though they were surely familiar enough, the absence of an organ does not prove that it was unknown. A second point of interest in the Plan is that although barely a sixth of the area was open to the *plebes*, there is a clear entrance for them at the west end, between the towers (where bells would be) and into a circulating space (where an organ might be).

A final point to note about the *Plan of St Gall* is that workshops were indicated, including those for such craftsmen as woodworkers (coopers or *tornatores*), leatherworkers *(fellarii)*, blacksmiths *(fabri)* and goldsmiths *(aurifices*, meaning also coppersmiths and tinsmiths?). These were men who, whether full-time lay craftsmen or brothers on a workshop rota, could have contributed in one way or another to the making of an organ, had their monastery wanted one. They needed only someone knowing from experience or from books how to calculate the relative lengths of pipes.

Problems with the Evidence

There are several puzzlng things about documentation before 1250 or so, both concerning actual organs and the way they were used. The most puzzling must be: Why are there not more references to either?

If, as seems plausible, there was an organ in several of the great monasteries across Francia from Jumièges to Prüm that were sacked by the Norsemen in the later ninth century, why is there no record of any of them? Perhaps the words of the music-theorist Hucbald, written at much the same period and in the same monastic area, are sufficient evidence that there were or had been actual instruments in this particular stretch of great monasteries (see p. 101). If so, his remarks on the compass of organs could imply that someone somewhere was skilled enough in metalwork and woodwork to make such things. Equally, those remarks could have inspired someone somewhere to try to make one. *Something* informed tenth-century organ-builders in England.

It is a fair starting-point to assume that theorists of music usually come after the event and not before, observing practice and trying to give the rationale for why singers or instrument-makers do as they do. Assuming for the moment that Hucbald is speaking from practical experience, then those monasteries sacked by the Vikings did quite possibly have an organ. But why is nothing said about them even when, as at St-Riquier, there is good documentation about other pieces of liturgical equipment made use of in its grand public events? This after all is the key period and key area in the musical development of the Western Church – northern Francia in the late ninth century – and here in particular one would expect references to *organa*. But there are none other than Hucbald.

One conclusion might be this: the organ was known, and it may have been placed in the church itself, but it had no part in the liturgy and instead served other functions of the monastery church. Churches were centres of pilgrimages, depositories of wonderful things, centre-points for various kinds of public ceremony, and places of instruction not least for the monks and not least in musical matters. Several of these functions would have been excellently served by a piece of apparatus which not only had a properly regulated and fixed scale sounded by pipes, but had also been made for the purpose, with the backing of a written-up theory of music. It was not referred to in documents because it was not necessary to the liturgy or to the apostolic mission of the monastery.

A further and related question is: How is it that there are certain groups of references but not others? One finds reports of organs in Carolingian annals around 800 but not a century later, English references of the tenth century but not the eleventh, chance references in the twelfth century but no systematic record, various reports of *organa* but no clear indication whether this means instruments (including the organ?) or ensemble music (including the organ?). And so on. In the case of the Anglo-Saxon organs there does seem to be an active interest at the end of the tenth century in mentioning special equipment, and one can speculate on what might have happened had hard times not followed in the wake of further trouble with the Danish kings. But the known references give little indication of how much people understood about instrument-making, and are inconsistent even for the four Saxon abbeys with known organs. In his prose *Life of St Æthelwold* (PL 137.92) Wulfstan himself says nothing about the bishop's organ and bell-wheel at Abingdon known about from other documentation (see above, p. 60), although he is at pains to recount the saint's achievements here and at Winchester.

Where organs are not mentioned even in material dealing with the crafts themselves, is it safer to assume that they were unknown? Here too the truth is elusive. The monks of Montecassino in the eleventh century, trained in metalwork and woodwork and in direct contact with Constantinople for major bronzework, were quite capable of making organs, but concrete reports of their skills by Bishop Desiderius make no mention of them (see Davis-Weyer: 135f). This is so even though he gives details of comparable metalwork, such as the silver crown-candelabrum which was a bringer of light for grand events in church just as organs were bringers of sound. Since it was another six or seven centuries before southern Italy developed much of an interest in organ-building, it could be that Montecassino and the south simply did not follow the habits of northern Benedictine houses. If this were so, it is all the more striking that this abbey has left the only example of vocal organum known from southern Italy during Desiderius's period.[13]

In the case of a northern monastery such as at Hildesheim, where a century earlier similar crafts had been documented, but again without mentioning instruments, organs might also have been known. This was an area as aggressively evangelical as it was advanced in its church-design, and it is near Hildesheim both in earlier times (Charlemagne's abbey at Corvey) and later (Theophilus's abbey at Helmarshausen) that one can safely imagine the ingenious Saxons developing their mechanical skills. At neither Montecassino nor Hildesheim, however, would the organ be essential equipment for the liturgy in the way that the silver chalice or the gospel-book was, and even had it been used occasionally in services it would not have been there exclusively

---

[13] A brief but interesting example of two-part counterpoint combining the 'white notes' in various intervals is reproduced by Kelly. At this period Montecassino also possessed a copy of the century's most influential book on music theory, the *Micrologus* of Guido d'Arezzo.

for that purpose. Is that the reason it is not mentioned?

Another key question is: Were those occasions on which *organa* of one kind or another are occasionally mentioned – e.g. the dedication of the monastery at Bages in 972, the consecration of the archbishop at Cologne in 953 – quite unusual (hence these references to them) or quite normal (hence so few other references elsewhere)? What records do exist suggest the latter rather than the former. Thus while one English monastery (Ramsey) had jubilant psalms, responses, hymns and organ at its dedication in 992, a report of the ceremony welcoming the new abbot of a far grander neighbouring monastery nearly two centuries later (Peterborough) mentioned none of these things, and said only this:

cum magna processione . . .	with a great procession . . .
a conuentu in propria	he was welcomed by the convent
sede Burgi susceptus est.	in his own seat of Peterborough.
(Mellows 1949: 127)	

But such an *adventus* – or at least the *Te deum* and mass celebrated as the new abbot took his seat in the church – must have been common. It was also an occasion traditionally associated with *organa*, certainly by this time in eastern England, as at Bury St Edmunds in 1182.

Most occasions of this sort do not get reported on at all in surviving chronicles, and it is probably fair to suspect that when there is a fuller report of such an event, one mentioning organs and bells, there may well be a particular reason for it. Thus at St Albans in 1235 there had been a power struggle involving both king and pope over electing the new abbot of this wealthy house (see RBMAS 28 and 57), and a careful record of the ceremony was clearly meant to establish the election's legitimacy. Hence the account of ceremonial noise and the singing of the *Te deum*, for these signalled acceptance of the new abbot in the sight of God and man. In this respect, reporting on an organ in the thirteenth century can have been as 'political' an act as it had been in the Carolingian kingdom half a millennium earlier.

If the appearance of an organ on such special occasions is usually difficult to prove, it is more difficult still to be certain when or how it was heard on regular occasions in the normal church year. A customary of St Augustine's Abbey, Canterbury (the manuscript itself from the second quarter of the thirteenth century), specifies some eleven festivals on which the organ played:[14] Christmas Day, St John the Evangelist, St Thomas Becket, Epiphany, St Hadrian, Octave of St Hadrian, Purification, Annunciation, Easter Day, St Michael, Translation of St Augustine (after the procession – i.e. the organ in church after the procession outside?). But quite apart from its being unclear what the organ actually played, one can only guess how far back beyond the twelfth century some such plan stretched. Since the list is still rather small, the answer might be: as long as there had been organs. This customary makes it at least possible that St Augustine's, Canterbury, had an organ at the period, as no doubt did comparable major abbeys elsewhere, but most of them no more recorded its presence than any other known document from this particular monastery did.

The Example of Notre-Dame Organum

So far in this section various English monasteries have been considered, but naturally a vast number of major institutions on the Continent are equally open to conjecture. None can be of greater musical interest than Notre-Dame, Paris, for it was here in the late twelfth century that the most developed repertory of notated vocal music or polyphony originated (the 'Notre Dame organum school'), in a cathedral of unusually majestic size and of unusual public and municipal significance. Processional responses in the grand polyphonic form were sung in front of the quire screen 'on at least a dozen major feasts of the year', and yet no organ is mentioned before 1332, leading to the conclusion that 'in fact there was no organ in Notre Dame prior to the fourteenth century' (Wright: 267, 143).

Now, were it certain that Notre-Dame did have no organ before 1332, interesting conclusions could be made, such as that even the most important of the period's great gothic non-monastic cathedrals were slow to take on an instrument long associated with Benedictine monasteries and with their kind of showy ceremony. But it is not certain. Much more likely is that there was an organ and that whether or not it was located near the quire, it was a piece of special noise-making

[14] Thompson, vol. 2, 293–4 (feastday list) and 261, 268 (concerning vespers and mass).

apparatus heard on a few festive occasions when the people (*plebes*) were thronging the church. Either way, it would not have been strictly liturgical, and probably did not play a part in the vocal music, either the large set-pieces of organum or the psalms and other chanted texts. The idea that the long-held notes in Notre-Dame vocal music of *c*.1200 were played by any instrument does not yet appear to be more than a guess.

While various of these points are still open, two things are certain about the reference of 1332. First, it does not imply anything unusual, unexpected or at all noteworthy about the organ, which would be strange if it were new or had not been preceded by an earlier instrument. And second, this and later references to the organ appear in the kinds of source (accounts, minutes, contractual documents) that simply did not exist in any systematic way earlier. If such documents had never come about, we would still not know of the organ of 1332. Of course, such an argument as this does not mean that early references to the vocal music (organum) of Notre-Dame have anything to do with any organ in the cathedral; rather, the point is that instrument and music are separate issues and that neither says anything about the other over the period concerned.

Nor is it likely that Notre-Dame was unusual in this respect. By the late twelfth century a great church could have possessed either an organ or a collection of sophisticated music for trained singers (written-down polyphony referred to in the documents as organum) – or, most likely, both. But the two need have had nothing to do with each other, despite the convention by which instrument and music had the same name. When a church left little if any documentation concerning either one of them, whichever it was, there can be no certainty that it was unfamiliar or actually unknown, for more churches surely knew both polyphony and instruments than documents now suggest. Once again, one needs to see that evidence as it exists may not say quite what it appears to say, while evidence that does not exist has to be replaced by deductions made from the few tangible witnesses that there are. If this is true about the mere presence of organs and about the way they were used, how much more true it is about the kind of sound they made and what they were like!

5

What Were Early Organs Like?

There remain technical questions about organs themselves, none of which is any more easily answered than those about how organs came to be there or what they did. As in the case of the pre-Christian organ, to approach any understanding at all involves specialized discussion of such technicalities as 'pipe-scales' and 'pallet-springs', metal-alloys and chest-construction, organ-choruses and manual keys. But the reader with some knowledge of organological language already will realize that much of what follows only confirms how uncertain one can be about the steps leading to those colourful, awe-inspiring instruments drawing the eyes and ears of the crowds in the great churches of Europe, at the end of the fifteenth century and on the eve of the Reformation.

Further on the Evidence

Whatever one assumes on seeing a picture of an early Christian organ, it is possible that *no actual instrument* is being portrayed in any kind of representation before the fourteenth century, if then; and whatever one assumes on seeing early, technically worded accounts of organs, it is possible that *no actual instrument* was being referred to, except in the concrete descriptions by Wulfstan and Theophilus (see below), if then. Although pictures and references in general have usually been treated in the past as positive sources of information, both will have depended to various degrees on what was drawn or written before, and both are as likely to have been abstract as actual (to use these words in a modern sense). All the sources had aims which influenced their information and in some way lessened it. It is therefore very difficult to guess what early organs were like, what they lost and what they gained, and the best one can do is weigh the evidence for their various characteristics.

A conspicuous example of the kind of medieval writing still frequently misinterpreted is the group of little treatises concerned with the proportional measurement of organ-pipes, how to understand it and (perhaps) how to apply it practically. This is a branch of music study based on Pythagoras's observation that, all things being equal, pitch will vary in relation to mass: the longer the pipe, the deeper the sound. Not until recently has it been fully shown that these little treatises were not prototype handbooks on how to make an organ, and that they had little in common with the technical manual now familiar to many kinds of reader. Rather, they were texts for the study of 'the art of music' *(ars musica)*, up to a point comparable to those written for study in the other mathematical liberal arts of arithmetic, geometry and astronomy. *Ars musica* had much the same relationship to organ-building and musical composition as geometry had to carpentry and house-building.

Nevertheless, these little treatises do contain some down-to-earth hints. The remark of the theorist Notker Labeo that like the string of a lira, an organ-pipe can be too long for its diameter and so produce only a 'hoarse' tone *(héisa* – Sachs 1970: 98) is a case in point. He or someone learned this from experience, and since so little is known about early organ-making, practical details of this kind need to be extracted from what theorists say and to be given their due weight.

Hints Given by Two Early Theorists

The oldest 'real' references to an organ in the work of a Western musician seem to be in a book on *musica* written towards the end of the ninth century by a monk of northern Francia, Hucbald.[1] Focusing on an issue of great importance to the organist – the layout of notes on his instrument – Hucbald refers to a keyboard with the following compass:

---

[1] GS 1.112b; also in Babb: 23ff.

Example 5

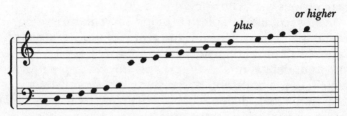

and says that the organ begins with the same notes as the cithara, an instrument of six strings. Isidore of Seville (†636) had also spoken of the cithara, but Hucbald's discussion cannot mean that he was only following in literary footsteps since his tuning-details are different and more specific. Besides, for such an author there is no simple separation between reading and observing: he uses his practical experience to develop what earlier books had said, in effect updating Isidore's brief remarks and establishing a way of looking at scales and instruments for monastic readers. They too knew the earlier books.

In pointing out that instruments use a different compass from voices (whose scale begins with the notes of a 'minor scale', from A), Hucbald is speaking not only of theory but is implying something about practice: beginning with the notes C D E F G A, organs of the day, like string instruments, could well have had a natural tendency towards 'music in C major'. Of course he does not put it in these terms, but observations on compass are none the less evocative, the more so if Hucbald is referring to actual string and/or wind instruments he knew. Since he also remarks that the B-flat then being recognized by theorists as a distinct note in the scale is 'however unlikely to be found on the organ or other instruments' (*quo tamen ydraulia vel organalia minime admisso*), it rather looks as if he is.

By *ydraulia*, Hucbald means not the water-organ but organ as distinct from other instruments: all instruments are *organa*, but like the others such as tuba, cithara and lira, the organ needed its own word. It played some kind of music based on the notes C D E F G A, though one cannot know with what agility, since Hucbald does not, and would not in such a book, describe the playing mechanism. Furthermore – and this was ultimately of even greater importance than what the starting-note of the scale was – Hucbald's compass was long enough to show the reader, or someone who could get to a keyboard to try it out, that the scale of music consists of successive octaves, as many as art required or technology could supply. As on no other instrument, one can *see* octaves on a keyboard, especially if the keys are labelled.

Compared to the conjectures inspired by Hucbald's remarks, the various little treatises that dealt with pipe-measurement or *mensura fistularum* are terse and basic. A particularly valuable source of information is the text *Cuprum purissimum* (Sachs 1970: 55–8), probably originating in Benedictine England or France as an insertion in a book on architecture, and becoming familiar as part of a treatise later called the 'Bern Anonymous' (eleventh century). Versions of the treatise circulated for some centuries, and many an interested reader would have followed its description of 'the purest copper' being worked with hammers 'to the utmost thinness' and rolled around a cylindrical iron mandrel almost four feet long, making a pipe and foot from the same length of copper. How one sheet of copper can produce both pipe and foot is not explained, and it is possible that the author was guessing from inexpertly observed pipes. In turn, however, this would mean that somewhere, somebody was making organ-pipes such as an author would want to describe.

The pipe-lengths given are those for a sequence of notes 'in which modern melodies mostly lie'. *Modern* probably means 'music composed or sung since the time of Pythagoras', such as chant which needed the notes of scales created by correct proportions. It looks as if the author or compiler was contributing to the traditional interest of Carolingian monasteries in theorizing about the notes of music and in making it possible, among other things, to classify the church's chant. The compass seems to have fifteen notes:

A B C D E F G A B C D E F G H
(here B = B-natural and H probably = a')

This is conventional vocal scale, not Hucbald's organ scale, and need not indicate an actual organ-compass, particularly since fifteen was a common number in scale-theory from the Greeks onwards. Either way, the keys are labelled, presumably for the same reason as in Theophilus's treatise (see below, p. 123).

The author continues by pointing out that the work involved in making a water-organ was more difficult than that for a bellows-organ, which need suggest no more than that he had read or heard of Vitruvius's *De architectura*. Remarks on the chest *(capsa)*, where the pipes are equidistantly placed, sound like passive observation, as if the author had seen an organ but was not certain either how the wind was dispersed inside the chest to each pipe or how he could describe its being so. As to the bellows: each pair is socketed into a wind-collector of the kind drawn in one later French manuscript (the Harding Bible), which strengthens the idea that this particular organ-treatise originated in northern France or, alternatively, that the Harding Bible artist had read it or something related to it.

An important part of the treatise concerns another visible part of the organ, the key-sliders[2] or *linguae,* fixed into the chest towards its top. How, it does not say, but probably they were perforated strips of wood pushed and pulled between the top boards of the chest below the pipes; or they were copper strips working through a solidified lead table (which would soon have worn) filling the top of the chest and bored with wind-channels up to the pipes. 'The rest of the apparatus' is the organ's key-action: on pressing a little wooden plate or key *(lamina lignea)* to which the slider is attached, the player pushes the slider in and so admits wind to the pipe, while a spring (a piece of elastic horn to which it is also attached) pulls it out again. This is in effect a mechanical system. (For further on sliders, see the summary of Vitruvius in chapter 2.)

Since this key-action is similar to that of the *hydraulis* described by Hero (see chapter 2), one wonders whether Hero texts circulated in the West in a translation now unknown, or whether they were only one of several sources of such information. In any case, if organs with returning keys were wanted in the tenth century, an organ-builder would know enough about springs of horn, iron or bronze to work out a design using them. Roman terracottas, Greek and

---

[2] On sliders and their various principles of construction, see above, p. 19.

Arabic treatises, tenth-century Christian descriptions – all suggest that craftsmen were quite capable of devising various kinds of keyboard, i.e. an ordered row of returning or non-returning levers (or sliders) acting on (or as) valves admitting and cutting off wind to the pipes.

'From the right of the one playing, to his left' the pipes on the chest increase in size; thus bass lies to the left. This too sounds like something the author saw, hardly a point for professionals, although it does confirm that the row of keys is in sequence. In fact, this is the oldest description in words of what is normally taken for granted with keyboards but is not inevitable.

The number of pipes per key can be as many as one pleases, five or ten or 'whatever' *(quotlibet)*, but they are to be only 'simple and duple' *(simplae et duplae)*, presumably meaning only unisons and octaves. This is a most important piece of information, though how it was obtained is not known. Did the author see an organ in which each key sounded five pipes but was told that it could be ten or more, or had he seen larger organ-chests for himself?

Other Treatises

After Theophilus, the modest treatise *Cuprum purissimum* is the most informative of the medieval texts. Although the fine discussion of note-proportions in a text attributed to Gerbert of Aurillac and Rheims (†1003) is realistic in its calculation of the width as well as length of pipes, it barely relates to actual instruments. The problem with such medieval work is to estimate what importance the writer put on actuality: Gerbert may have known of the 'note-names with which our organs are marked' only from books and not personal experience, and it is also possible that the second was less important than the first. But while his references to *organa* in connection with the abbeys (or the abbots) of Bobbio, Aurillac and Fleury may relate to 'teaching-aids' for the science of music rather than to actual organs in church (or in these churches), it would not mean that they were any the less significant for his purposes, which was to describe how to calculate an orderly scale of notes.[3]

---

[3] For the remark on the note-names, see Sachs 1970: 65 (a *mensura* treatise); for references to Bobbio, Aurillac and Fleury, see Sachs 1972 (Gerbert's letters).

In texts associated with William, Abbot of Hirsau (†1091), practical experience is very specific and therefore credible: the treatise *Primae ergo* lays out the scale for a compass of

Example 6

and adds that above this the pipes become shrill *(absonae fiunt)* and below it impossible to blow *(perflari nequeunt)*, as 'we have tested' *(probavimus* – Sachs 1970: 85). Any such experience must have been with actual pipes, but whether it was when another eleventh-century theorist, Aribo, gave other practical details about pipe-making – soldering with tin, pressing in the mouth and making the windway as wide as a straw (Sachs 1970: 92) – is not at all certain. At best, he could have been making observations on something made by a craftsman using methods he knew nothing about.

Bits of information about how many pipes there were per key also occasionally emerge, as again in Aribo (*c*.1070), who speaks of

quot choros fistularum	as many choruses of pipes as
musici solent ipsi organico	musicians are themselves used to
instrumento apponere et	put in the *organic* instrument and
ad organizandi artem habere.	to have for the art of *organizing*.
(Sachs 1970: 126)	

Whatever the precise meaning of *choros* here, and whether *organizandi* means anything more specific than 'organ-playing', the keys seem to have more than a single pipe each. Since Aribo may have been another writer from southern Germany, it looks as if the habit of referring to technical details, however vague they may seem to later readers, is likely to have arisen there earlier or more often than it is elsewhere.

The early treatise or text beginning *Mensuram et* (Sachs 1970: 95), also circulating in English copies of the twelfth century, specifies that an octave pipe 'be placed between two larger' on the chest *(inter duas maiores fistulas ponatur)*. This means that for each key there are three pipes, two at the unison and one at the octave, arranged from front to back in the order unison-octave-unison (or 8.4.8).[4] Also, the pipe-measurements for one set of seven or eight notes can be extrapolated to two or three further sets, therefore making a compass of fifteen or twenty-one notes. All this may well be another sign of practical experience on the author's or somebody's part, for placing an octave pipe between two unisons helps prevent interference in the air between mouths of pipes at the same height.[5] And what could be done for three ranks of pipes could be done for any number.

A mention in the south German text *Longissimam* of 'instruments which are put into action by water' *(organis . . . quae ad aquam moventur* – Sachs 1970: 97) does not prove that water-organs were still in use or even much understood at the time, for the words are taken from Boethius. *Longissimam* was copied about 1000 and is one of a family of texts partly translated into the vernacular by Notker Labeo of St Gall (†1022?). A related text, *Fac tibi*, describes the make-up of notes per key in more detail (Sachs 1970: 115):

the notes C D E F have pipes at unison, octave and super-octave (8.4.2)
the notes G A B-flat B-natural have unison and octave (8.4.4 or 8.8.4?).[6]

This is the first known reference to the principle of 'breaking back', i.e. small pipes doubling in length (and thus falling back an octave) at the point in the rising scale when they would otherwise become too short. If the author meant these eight notes C to B-natural to stand for a longer compass, he

[4] 8 = a pipe at unison pitch, 4 = the octave above, 16 = the octave below, etc.
[5] Vortices are produced in the air at the point at which the sound originates, thus inside and outside the upper lip of the pipe-mouth; those curling on the outside could interfere with those of another mouth nearby.
[6] Not until the fourteenth century, and then not unambiguously, are fifth-sounding or quint ranks referred to in a pipe-measurement treatise; see Sachs 1980: 335ff.

would be saying that smaller pipes change about once every octave, therefore at several points in a longer keyboard.

That an organ-builder might like to go to three octaves and above is mentioned in more than one twelfth-century text,[7] and although such observations could be made purely as a matter of theory, they do describe a plausible organ. St Gall had a history of intense scribal activity in recording endowments and in training monastic scribes in the German vernacular,[8] and it may also have encouraged practical, technical work over a wide region of lively central European monasteries.

Hints in Medieval Drawings

Also problematic is deciding what is actual or practical in the handful of early representations of organs, seldom well drawn but often reproduced today. Very large bibliographies have been created on the question of what information it is that the early Utrecht and Stuttgart Psalters (both c.820/830) are conveying, but it would be a mistake to assume that much later drawings, such as the various psalters of the fourteenth century, necessarily give a more 'actual' picture of organs.

One of the manuscripts best known to musicians, the *Utrecht Psalter*[9] probably originated in Hautvillers, a monastery near Rheims and thus in the same stretch of Carolingian-Benedictine France as Hucbald's. More than in any other known psalter, music and instruments form a major theme of its celebrated line-drawings, and many suggestions have been made about their origin, in particular whether they came from life, books or earlier drawings. (See also p. 39 for the Psalter's possible connection with other documents of c.830.) Assuming that the Psalter's psalms were illustrated in order, the sketch in the drawing for Psalm 70/71 may be the oldest manuscript illustration of an organ. A few ink-lines suggest either nine or seven pipes, a shallow chest and two water-cisterns with hoops. The drawing looks unfinished, but

---

[7] Or copy of an earlier text: e.g. Sachs 1970: 124.
[8] Some discussion in Sachs 1980: 200.
[9] For recent facsimile and commentary, see Horst.

its apparent carelessness is a means of conveying the psalm's *topos*: King David was indifferent to man-made instruments.

In the fuller and famous picture for Psalm 150, a firm (wooden?) base supports four pistons-and-cylinders with hinged levers worked reciprocally by four energetic blowers using both arms, and these feed two round water-cisterns bound with hoops. From these cisterns a neck passes into a shallow chest on which are placed two identical rows of four or five graded pipes, treble to the player's right. Two organists stand behind, the first with the fingers of both hands doing something on the chest, the second with one hand similarly placed while the other directs (beats time for?) two blowers. Blowers and players are producing sound not in a church service but in a cosmic scene of praise ('let everything that hath breath'); other participating instruments include horns, perhaps representing a tradition for coupling organs and horns known since the days of Roman mosaics.

In the normal way, the pressure and volume of wind produced by such pistons would feed far more than four or five organ-pipes, and one can imagine various explanations for the discrepancy: for example, the pipes speak at very high pressure: four stands for a bigger row or more than one row: they express the artist's understanding of the tetrachord and are therefore a visual synecdoche, like the seven notes in other medieval illustrations of organs or string instruments. Some interpreters have also assumed the players to be Christian monks, robed and tonsured, but comparison with other figures in the Psalter makes this unlikely.

One likely connection between the drawing and older psalm-commentaries is the strange way in which the organists are threading their fingers through the pipes: perhaps the artist was relying on the words of Cassiodorus (see p. 24), whose mention of mechanism is so brief that the reader (including the present artist?) is left to guess what a player actually did. As to why there are two organists: although some corroboration for the idea appears in Wulfstan's poem at Winchester (see p. 120), the Utrecht picture is planned symmetrically so that there are two or multiples of two for all figures in it except God Almighty in the centre.

The third picture of an organ in the Utrecht Psalter is for

the apocryphal Psalm 151, which speaks of David as shepherd and musician, making an *organum* and playing a *psalterium* (v. 2). The drawing shows a similar water-organ. This time the player is looking towards the king, not unlike the watchful *hydraulis*-player in gladiatorial mosaics – again an antique detail, as if in the right circumstances a barbaric practice could be converted to a sacred. Or perhaps the artist knew what organ-players looked like only from an old mosaic?

The *Stuttgart Psalter*[10] may have been made at much the same time in another northern French scriptorium (St Germain-des-Près, Paris?). Large bellows-organs are painted with some convincingly real detail for Psalms 150 and '151' – perhaps a direct interpretation by the artist of words of St Augustine, as the unclear wooden key-action was also suggested by the unclear words of Cassiodorus? For Psalm 150 there are wind, percussion and string instruments, joined by a dancer and three (?) bellows-blowers, two of whom tread a bull- or goatskin bellows. This is of the whole-skin type described by Theophilus, known far and wide for many centuries and used for many purposes. The third figure may be treading a second skin-bellows or playing the organ; or he is there to bring to eight the number of persons about King David, representing the eight musical forms of praise. The chest is shallow and seems to be made up of joined timber members (a most important detail), and the blowers have their hand on a bar – surely a realistic detail, though whether such support-bars were as familiar for organ-bellows in church as they were for forge-bellows outside is not known.

Two other psalms are illustrated with organs: Psalm '151' has a similar instrument to Psalm 150, while Psalm 136/137 ('By the rivers of Babylon') has a pair of little organs hanging in trees. The idea for these may well have come from some other source, including the illustrator's own imagination, but pan-pipes are sometimes shown hanging in foliage in pagan Roman sculpture, as they are too for Psalm 136/137 in many a Greek psalter. (For St Jerome on this psalm and its organs, see above, p. 23.) The Babylon organs have seven (?) pipes

[10] For recent facsimile and commentary, see Stuttgart.

each, six or seven little key-tabs below the pipes, a frame and an oblique bar across the pipe-rows. Such *organetti* could be fantasy, a miniaturization conjectured by the artist from the larger organs, or he could have known Greek psalters in which some such motif was conventional.

One thing to bear in mind when sources of an artist's knowledge are so nebulous is that the situation cannot have been so different for the organ-builders themselves. Particularly if they were monastic craftsmen making instruments, they too would be able to use their imagination in working wood, metal and leather. In addition, as literate brothers they too knew illustrated psalters and could get the idea of miniature organs from what various artists had conjured up in their drawings. By definition, psalters were books of authority.

In the centuries after these two psalters, the representations become if anything less 'actual' through artists observing conventions that had become fixed for each kind of picture. Thus the *Pommersfelden* and *Harding Bibles* (second half of the eleventh century, and *c*.1109) picture David and the four musicians who customarily represent wind, percussion and string instruments, and although these organs have two ranks of pipes (cylindrical, conical) and a row of sliders, no 'real' detail is necessarily being conveyed. This type of drawing has its conventions irrespective of 'reality', and in the case of the Harding Bible, the eight sliders, note-labels and bellows-structure may well come from written descriptions. A further iconographical programme informs a David picture in the *Cambridge Psalter* (early twelfth century),[11] where animals around the throne allude to verses in the Old Testament quite as much as those actually carved and made to roar in the throne-room of the Palace at Constantinople (see p. 30).

Since drawings of organs are so few in the total mass of early medieval illustration, it must be significant when they are admitted to an established genre such as *David and his Musicians*. No genre need be more 'reliable factually' than another, but in the later thirteenth century, as written documentation expanded to include new forms, so did iconology: unfamiliar types of scenes, often in the margins of

[11] Reproductions in Perrot 1971: Utrecht = plate XXIV, Pommersfelden, Harding and Cambridge = plate XXV.

the manuscripts, bring new details and show more 'real' features. In its David scene, the *Belvoir Psalter*[12] gives the first picture of a keyboard in the sense of a row of about twenty-two square keys moving up and down, or hinged at the distal end of the lever. The picture may have meant to show that nimble, individual fingers could operate keys, and that these keys return automatically to position – or was King David, by definition, able to do things no one else could?

Keyboards appear in other late thirteenth-century manuscripts and gradually become a normal part of organs when these are drawn or painted from close by. By the mid-fifteenth century keyboards have become a feature important enough – alluding to the period's miraculously efficient mechanisms, perhaps? – as to be prominent in the two well-known oil-paintings of Van Eyck and Van der Goes. These pictures appear to be as accurate as a photograph, and are still often claimed to be so, but in fact they are straightforwardly reliable neither as to their keyboard nor their row of pipes. In neither picture does the keyboard even seem to correspond to the pipes.

In comparison to keyboards, bellows are often realistically drawn. This suggests two things: not only that they were more familiar to artists of the period but that artists were capable of drawing 'reliably' when they were familiar enough with the object.

The Most Complete Remains: Aquincum, c.225

Before the late Middle Ages, drawings are occasionally matched by written evidence but hardly at all by actual physical remains. Earlier, and in whatever connection one is speaking, guesses need to be made about what it was men could make with their hands, not only because documentation and archaeology supply little evidence but because what evidence there is gives two different pictures. For example, nothing in the Greek-Roman descriptions of water-pumps suggests that they could be made from a length or two of lead piping held in an ingeniously bored-out wooden block, complete with valves and a receiver. But this is exactly the form of

[12] Perrot 1971: plate XXVII, also called *The Rutland Psalter*.

a pump found in the Roman *civitas* capital of Silchester (Usher: 87–8), and it seems unlikely that Roman Britain had something other provinces did not.

Similarly, nothing in Vitruvius or Hero leads one to expect the kind of Roman organ excavated at Aquincum, Budapest, earlier this century. This is a tiny thirteen-note organ made in the early third century, with a chest-top of 27×8 cm, spring-loaded key-sliders and four rows of bronze pipes; three of the rows may have had stopped pipes (see Kaba and Walcker-Mayer). It is uncertain whether it was blown with bellows or by means of a water-cistern, but its weight would not have made it easily portable even if it had had small bellows. Some details of this instrument are:

The spruce chest was lined inside and out with soldered bronze plates. Key-sliders (with four holes) are of thick cast bronze, as are the four longitudinal sliders (was this after all what Vitruvius meant? – see p. 17).

Narrow-scaled pipes made of thin bronze sheets, three ranks with oak stoppers, one open, standing firm in deep rings soldered on the chest. It is possible that pipes were changeable: for the stopped ranks, the upper sections fit separately into the feet and could be replaced.

The keyboard: a metal hook seems to have pulled out the end of the metal slider, a hook operated probably not by hand but by an elmwood key (some 1.4 cm wide) attached to it. The slider was pushed back by a bronze leaf-spring set vertically at the front of the organ. Quick reiteration of a note cannot have been possible.

The ranks: the four different ranks appear to have had different pitches and/or tuning, perhaps with a compass of something like (in modern note-names) a b c′ d′ e′ f′ f#′ g′ a′ b′-flat c′ d′ e′ (at a pitch of c′ = 440Hz).

If the four ranks did provide different pitches or tunings, then this was not a screeching organ but a set of four flutes, with distinctive modal tunings used separately for (one would imagine) subtle, indoor music.

But if written descriptions do not lead one to expect the Silchester pump or the Aquincum organ, as is the case, nor do they forbid them. Together this pump and this organ are a good reminder that before the period of patents, written technical description was likely to be partial, giving principles rather than particular solutions such as they were devised by craftsmen, or such as they might have survived here and there. Written descriptions are concerned with mechanical models more difficult to make than would be obvious to a common craftsman, hence the conclusion, already proposed in Usher: 89, that the hydraulic organ described by Vitruvius and Hero was not the only type of organ known.

Without the Aquincum organ, this would be only a guess, but Aquincum shows two important things: that (fairly) simple ways to make an organ-structure could have been improvised locally; and that skilled metalworking could turn to the making of organ-pipes and to voicing them according to changing tastes.

The Most Complete Description: Wulfstan, c.990

Thirty lines of polished verse by a late tenth-century cantor, Wulfstan of Winchester, provide the most detailed account of a clearly identified organ before contracts began in the later fourteenth century.[13] A fascinating and unique document, the account leaves many uncertainties, not least whether the organ was as unique as the poem. The lines read:

141 *talia et auxistis hic organa, qualia nusquam*
    and you enlarged [endowed?] the organs here, such as are
    cernuntur, gemino constabilita solo.
    nowhere else seen, fixed on a double floor [on two levels].
    bisseni supra sociantur in ordine folles,
    Twice six bellows are joined above in a row,
    inferiusque iacent quattuor atque decem.
    and below lie four and ten.
145 *flatibus alternis spiracula maxima reddunt.*
    With alternating breaths [vents?] they render a great
        amount of air.
    quos agitant ualidi septuaginta uiri

---

[13]Text from Campbell: 69–70. These are lines 141–72 of a 588-line narrative in verse, consisting of a prologue and *Life* of St Swithun, Bishop of Winchester (†862), and dedicated to Æthelwold's successor at Winchester, Bishop Alphege (†1012), later Archbishop of Canterbury and martyr.

Which [bellows] seventy strong men work,
brachia uersantes, multo et sudore madentes,
moving their arms and dripping with much sweat,
certatimque suos quique monent socios,
each eagerly encouraging his companions
uiribus ut totis impellant flamina sursum,
to drive the air upward with all strength
150 *et rugiat pleno kapsa referta sinu,*
and make roar the full chest with its ample curve [or: from
   the full reservoir],
sola quadringentas, quae sustinet ordine musas,
which by itself supports the four hundred muses in order,
quas manus organici temperat ingenii:
which the hand of organic skill controls:
has aperit clausas, iterumque has claudit apertas,
it opens the closed and in turn closes the opened,
exigit ut uarii certa Camena soni,
as the prescribed song [or: chant] of diverse notes requires,
155 *considuntque duo concordi pectore fratres,*
and two brothers of harmonious spirit sit together,
et regit alphabetum rector uterque suum,
and each, like a ruler, rules his alphabet,
suntque quaterdenis occulta foramina linguis,
and there are hidden openings in four times ten tongues,
inque suo retinet ordine quaeque decem.
and each holds ten in its own rank [in due order?].
huc aliae currunt, illuc aliaeque recurrunt,
Hither some tongues run, thither some return,
160 *servantes modulis singula puncta suis,*
serving the individual holes in their own places [the
   separate holes in the chest according to their pitches?]
et feriunt iubilum septem discrimina uocum,
and the 'seven separate voices' strike up the jubilant song,
permixto lyrici carmine semitoni,
mixed additionally with the song of the lyric semitone.
inque modum tonitrus uox ferrea uerberat aures,
And in the manner of thunder the iron voice beats upon
   the ears
preter ut hunc solum nil capiant sonitum,
that they receive no sound beyond only this.
165 *concrepat in tantum sonus hinc illincque resultans,*

The sound so clamours, echoing here and there,
quisque manu patulas claudat ut auriculas,
that everyone closes the opening of his ears with his hand,
haudquaquam sufferre ualens propiando rugitum,
totally unable to bear the noise when drawing near,
quem reddunt uarii concrepitando soni,
which the various sounds produce in their clamouring.
musarumque melos auditur ubique per urbem,
And the melody of the pipes is heard everywhere in the city,
170 *et peragrat totam fama uolans patriam.*
and flying fame goes through the whole country.
hoc decus ecclesiae uouit tua cura tonanti,
It was your care that consecrated this glory of the church to
    [God] the Thunderer,
clauigeri inque sacri struxit honore PETRI.
and set it up in honour of the holy keybearer Peter.

The poem and the dedication of the enlarged Old Minster
are both dated 993/4, the organ therefore a little before. That
the poem written was concerned with the minster's rebuilding suggests that the organ was built or rebuilt at least in part
for the dedication ceremonies themselves.

Something particularly striking about the poem is that
even if it were not about an actual instrument but only
another elaborate allegory for the unity-in-diversity of a
Christian community – hence the 'if then' in the opening sen-
tences of this chapter – the word *organa* clearly means 'organ'
and not merely 'instruments' or 'psalters and gospels', much
less 'ensemble music'. Furthermore, such a description could
be both actual and symbolic, with no either/or about it. In
view of the poem's position and what it suggests about an
instrument in *c.*1000, each line deserves some scrutiny:[14]

Line 141. The organ was put up, perhaps 'enlarged'. The
possibility that Winchester did have an earlier organ raises
further questions about how long the instrument had been
known to the Anglo-Saxon Church and what it was like. A
guess would be that there had been a smaller instrument
made a few years previously at Winchester: as St Alphege

[14] It is a curious characteristic of these lines that they relate only to the organ,
doing so in such a way that it is impossible to extract from them.

enlarged his predecessor's crypt in the minster, so he did his *organum*. In addition, both crypt and organ would have been rebuilt partly for the sake of the lay people, the pilgrims and the royal city's constant train of aristocratic visitors.

Again, then, reference to a tenth-century organ has survived by chance, and again a hint is dropped that there had been makers producing such instruments long enough previously for an earlier organ to need enlarging.

Lines 141–2. Such organs were not otherwise known. This remark is much like that made about Pippin's Greek organ (see chapter 2), but the next phrase may imply what was new: it was not portable but fixed on two floors, a major instrument with bellows on one level and sounding parts above.

Lines 143–4. Here the impression given is of a double row of bellows linked to a windtrunk; if so, this would represent a stage of organ-building beyond that known to the Romans, though not necessarily to the Byzantines. It may also suggest that the builder had previous experience. Twenty-six hand-held wedge-bellows are not out of the question, pumped energetically in alternation (two bellows per man) by teams of blowers in shifts, hence the need for so many men.

But Wulfstan's figures cannot be relied upon simply because he was a cantor and must know what he was talking about. If, as well a poet might, he means simply 'a large group of men working together towards a common end', like the seventy translators of the Old Testament working for seventy days, then the unequal numbers of bellows and blowers is not a problem. But one occasion on which he may actually have needed five shifts of thirteen men each (plus a fourteenth man to 'spell' the alternating rhythm for each team) was the minster's dedication – a special occasion on which the organ sounded for much of the day as various parts of the structure and monastic grounds were consecrated and the bounds beaten. Otherwise, it is hard to believe that even as many as fourteen bellows-blowers were regularly gathered.

Line 145. Eager encouragement of the kind the blowers are described as exchanging would hardly be appropriate if they were in sight of the people or if the organ sounded during regular liturgy. Neither, therefore, was the case?

Lines 149–50. The wind is driven upward to the chest: Wulfstan's *referta* gives the impression of a chest crammed with mechanism or pipes much as a reliquary *(capsa)* would be crammed with bones. Each kind of *capsa* breathed forth to believers an intangible spirit.

Line 151. The idea of twenty-six bellows for only four hundred pipes is not easily convincing despite the plausibility of ten pipes for each key (i.e. with duplicated pitches). Perhaps 'four hundred' stands for 'a very large number'. But there is also another explanation for the poem's various numbers. Most could be found in, and would be reminders of, the Pentateuch: 2 (various pairs in Genesis), 7 (days of creation and rest), 10 (e.g. the decalogue), 40 (e.g. the wilderness years), 70 (e.g. the Elders), and 400 (representing the last letter of the Hebrew alphabet, a kind of summation). Since 70 might stand for the Septuagint translators, perhaps Wulfstan knew of some reckoning of the Hebrew books that made them number 26; or 26 was the number of books in the New Testament if he disregarded Jude.[15] Either way, seventy blowers working on twenty-six bellows were as seventy scribes working on twenty-six canonical books, and in both cases their 'message' resounded far and wide, as it was meant to.

Was all this an elaborate reference to the tenth-century reformers' takeover of the Old Minster at Winchester? The idea that in leading in regular monks to replace the slack clergy of Winchester, St Alphege or St Æthelwold was a Moses leading the Chosen of the Pentateuch into their rightful home, seems likely enough to inform a poem written by one of them.[16] Of course, the numbers of pipes and bellows could still have been actual and 'reliable', in which case it must be as commentators have said in the past: at Winchester the over-capacity of the bellows was necessary to help stabilize the supply of wind because the apparatus lost so much of it.

---

[15] It is surely coincidence that according to a French definition of 1395, a 'crowd' *(tourbe)* was constituted by the number twenty-six. F. Godefroy, *Dictionnaire de l'ancienne langue française*, 10 vols (Paris, 1880–1902), 7.748.
[16] Events of the Pentateuch mark the completion of Israel's captivity in Egypt and of the subsequent wanderings before the Chosen People enter the Promised Land. (The Book of Exodus also has forty chapters.)

Lines 152–3. Skill is 'organic' when it produces the notes of music calculated correctly. 'Opening' and 'closing' is more specific and may refer to sliders that have to be pulled out and pushed in, or to keys that operated them, spring-loaded or not. A pious allusion is also possible: the *organ* is the Church and the *ruler* is Jesus, the one 'that openeth and no man shutteth' (Revelation 3:7). This would agree with the idea of the Church as 'the organ of God' (see p. 41).

Line 154. *Certa* suggests something 'prescribed' – as distinct from the haphazardly produced jumble of sound from bells or the screech of an organ used for signalling? The mechanism can produce the basic sounds or notes of music, and these can be articulated melodically by the player.

Lines 155–60. Two brothers play forty slider-keys of ten holes each, and the keys are marked, actually or metaphorically, with a letter of music. A slider of ten holes is difficult to imagine, especially if the forty keys ran from bass to treble, for this would mean that in the bass there were large pipes taking more room on the chest and therefore needing yet longer sliders. More likely is that the slider had one large hole and that for each note there were ten pipe-holes on the chest. In turn, this would imply that Wulfstan did not know quite what a chest was like inside.

Several phrases in the poem imply some kind of double organ, with two organists and the two alphabets, and indeed the organ could have had a divided chest with twenty sliders in each half and two keyboards duplicating each other. A large-sized organ of ten rows of pipes is conceivable in which there were none larger than 4' or even 2': each row 'broke back' at a certain point, or each player's keyboard started at tenor or middle C. In neither case would there really be a 'bass', which also means there would be no characteristic of distinctive 'treble' either. Nevertheless, any such keyboard would have been able to play held notes, tone-clusters and the melody of the *Te deum*.

Lines 161–2. There are eight different notes. Taken literally, this agrees with the familiar alphabet C D E F G A B-flat B-natural and is an octave 'module' for any keyboard, the notes of the *septem discrimina vocum* of Virgil (*Aeneid* 6.646) plus one. The 'lyric semitone' is the note added to the seven strings of the classical lyre and is a fanciful reference to B-flat, evidently a note familiar to organ-makers before it was to music-theorists.[17]

Lines 163–70. The sound is thunderous. The language of passages to do with the organ's impression on the ear, including its blotting out other sound, is particularly allusive to the Latin poets. While some phrases are too commonplace to suggest anything but a well-read cantor, the reference to thunder is more specific and formulaic, ultimately traceable to the *Iliad* 2.478 and 2.781.

Lines 171–2. The organ is in honour of St Peter, therefore possibly placed near the saint's altar (see also p. 92).

Arguing from the poem's factual accuracy when it describes other parts of the church, one could interpret the poem as straightforwardly describing a double organ of four hundred pipes and two players. Such apparatus would reliably indicate what a reinvigorated abbey of the late tenth century had in the way of *organa*.

Assuming that Wulfstan did not think or intend to make others think that two-part music necessarily required two players – a cantor would surely know better – perhaps two players did work two sets of sliders. Unfortunately, the two symmetrical organists shown for Psalm 150 in the Utrecht Psalter cannot be seen as corroborating evidence for the idea, since Wulfstan may well have known the Psalter (in England by the late tenth century?) and had its two players in mind. Nevertheless, it is worth remembering that any tradition there was for seeing 'two concordant brothers' as a personification of Christian *harmony* need not have belonged exclusively to artists and poets: in exceptional instances an organ-builder might give concrete expression to the same idea. This would not mean that it was always necessary to use two players, any more than it was to employ a crowd of bellows-blowers on every occasion.

---

[17] A much later example of the 'lyric semitone' can be heard in Thomas Tallis's hymn 'Expend, O Lord, my plaint of word': the flattened seventh is the only accidental used in the hymn (where it is a regular *eighth note*), and emphasizes word-setting (e.g. 'musing'). The effect is harmonic, as is also the case with most folk-song idioms developed by more recent composers. An even later example of the lyric semitone used in a pseudo-folk melody (ultimately Scottish?) can be heard in Jay Ungar's fiddle tune *Ashokan Farewell* (*c.*1984).

Speculating beyond the poem, one can imagine the following: a large organ made either locally or by journeymen moving their workshop from one Saxon monastery to another, an instrument with a chorus of unisons and octaves based on pipes no bigger than 4', two rows of keys (side by side?) of twenty notes each (two and a half octaves), and a mechanism agile anough to allow several, perhaps all, of the musical techniques listed in chapter 4. It can only be guessed how long the Winchester organ was there to be heard. The Saxon abbey-cathedral was destroyed by the Norman bishop before the end of the eleventh century, and presumably any organs documented in the new Norman cathedral were new.

The Most Complete Treatise: Theophilus, c.1125

Not only is the so-called *De diversis artibus*, written between 1100 and 1140, quite the fullest technical treatise on the organ from the period during which the Christian Church adopted it, but it remained so for centuries afterwards (text in Dodwell).[18] Its author, the 'monk and priest Theophilus', has been identified with a goldsmith Rogkerus, who worked in the monastery of Helmarshausen some fifteen miles south of Corvey and seems to have lived previously in the Ardennes and at Cologne (the monastery of St Pantaleon). For many years this area, from the Meuse valley across the Rhine to Saxony, could well have been developing various metal technologies for church use, including many an undocumented bell and organ.

There are three sections in the treatise, the first on fine-art items, the second on windows, the third on large metalwork including organ (§81–4) and bells (§85, by far the largest chapter in the treatise). The author explains that with his treatise the reader will study those things – fine objects for church – that otherwise have to be imported at great trouble or learned about only at great pains. In some of its detail the treatise seems to look to the past, as if the author is observing an actual organ and surmising how it was made; other parts

---

[18] Why there is nothing comparable to it for another three hundred years, and then only fitfully for a further two hundred, is a big question deserving treatment elsewhere.

seem to be catering for new requirements, as when he offers advice on where to locate organs.

Perhaps precisely because Vitruvius barely mentions pipes in his treatise, Theophilus begins with a detailed description of how to make them. He assumes that some other text will give the maker exact dimensions from which to start, and in specifying only a few notes – 'seven or eight' grooves in the chest – he may well be leaving his whole description open to extrapolation. In other words, although Theophilus does not say so, skilled craftsmen could have used his directions to make a much larger instrument,[19] it being his concern to describe the principles of construction.

The pipe-metal is pure copper, beaten thin to produce a work-hardened sheet and rolled round an iron mandrel, the making of which is not described but was a major engineering feat. Especially if the pipe were conical, which is not certain, its thin hardened copper would produce a scratchy or breathy pipe-tone, perhaps like the coarse singing one could imagine for the period. In Book 3 §45, Theophilus describes a very similar method of manufacture for the small silver 'pipe' used with the communion chalice (a kind of drinking straw), and this was tapered. Such a chalice pipe, an item surely in great demand, was also described in an earlier and influential fine-art treatise,[20] and it must have afforded craftsmen the skill to make at least smaller organ-pipes. Conversely, one wonders whether organ-builders had other methods for making organ-pipes if or when they were not craftsmen engaged in making holy vessels in monastery workshops.

In speaking of a pipescale 'as one wishes' (qua vult), Theophilus can hardly mean 'any size whatsoever', for the bottom note, a nominal C, may have varied in pipe-length only between 3' and 4' (or any double or half thereof), as organ-builders would always have known. Each conical pipe-length is cut into at the point that the mouth will be, and the upper and lower edges of the mouth-slot are filed until the gap is as wide as a straw (festuca). Filing the mouths of copper

---

[19] Previous commentators have not examined this possibility.
[20] Soldered gold 'pipes' for such altar and communion-equipment are also described in the ninth-century handbook Mappae clavicula: A Little Key to the World of Medieval Sciences, ed. C. S. Smith and J. G. Hawthorne (Philadelphia, 1974).

pipes in this way means more labour than fine-cutting tin or lead pipes, hence perhaps the increasing use of pewter as organs became more common. In any case, it looks as if Theophilus was describing an actual pipe he had examined.

At this point in the process the pipe is still a springy sheet of copper, which is then fastened around the mandrel. Together they are then heated, and the mandrel has the effect of stabilizing the temperature. After the pipe has cooled, it is turned on a lathe to equalize stress in the copper and make smooth both the inner and (because it is so thin) the outer surfaces. The mouth is pressed in almost to the middle of the pipe, and the languid is soldered in.[21] One tests the pipe by blowing it first weakly, then strongly, then very strongly, and 'according to what one hears, one voices the pipe' (*secundum quod auditu discernit, disponat vocem*). These words surely suggest something that Theophilus had observed: opening the horizontal mouth-slit or windway makes the sound fuller (*grossam*), while narrowing it makes it less full (*graciliorem*).

The chest on which the pipes stand can be made of wood or of copper. The wooden is made from two thick planks of plane-tree wood, hollowed out and grooved with wind-channels, and then joined together by a casein glue described elsewhere in the treatise. (Such hollowing out of a block, both as a flat box and with the base surface domed, is the way in which all known early medieval fiddles and lyres were made. Plane-tree wood was recommended probably because it has little sap and is not too sensitive to damp.) The dimensions given by Theophilus are only enough for his 'module' organ of seven or eight notes. In the bottom of the upper plank the slider-keys are fitted to slide in and out easily without the wind escaping, but how they are made and fitted is not detailed, being a carpentry question.

'Seven or eight' presumably means with or without B-flat, and in any case the note-names (*litterae*) are written on the slider-ends. This is puzzling, for if the notes were so few, why was it necessary to label them? – perhaps because the player was not a regular organist and needed to be told where the

---

[21] Languid: the interior metal disc just below the mouth, almost closing off the pipe but cut so as to allow a thin sheet of wind to pass up to strike the upper lip.

semitones lay, something important when chant and vocal *organum* observed no standard pitch. The movement of the slider-keys is checked by a copper nail passing through a slot in them; the slot is about 1½" long, the key-travel therefore slightly less. This is an important detail about sliders, unique in the sources. There is no mention of springs and therefore whether the keys return to the rest-position by themselves.

In §84 directions are given for making a cast copper chest on the lost-wax technique, with dimensions 'according to the number of pipes'. The top of the chest is covered with a layer of molten lead through which the sliders eventually slide. This chapter also includes directions on a copper wind-collector (see next paragraph) and the copper valve for bellows,[22] and one has to assume that modest copper or bronze chests were still being made in the late eleventh century.

Two types of bellows are included by Theophilus elsewhere in Part 3 of his treatise: hand-held wholeskin bellows and (not detailed) the larger fold-bellows held in a rigid wooden frame, both used for forgework, fine or coarse. However, in the organ section a wooden wind-collector is described in some detail, i.e. a shaped box into which the bellows send their wind, constructed to be as airtight as possible. The trunk curving up from it to the chest was made from a well-chosen oak branch, hollowed out, the joints at either end covered with linen and further sealed with copper. Such a trunk of wood must have been more airtight than one of joined pieces, and some such curving windtrunk is clearly drawn in several early representations of organs.

Important suggestions are made on placing the instrument in church. 'So that nothing be seen below in the minster' (? – *infra monasterium*) except the 'pipes standing on the chest', the structure can be so planned that the pipechest is on the floor above the bellows. This must suggest that in some earlier organs the bellows and the bellows-blowers were all too visible, which in turn means that by Theophilus's time the instrument was becoming less of a mere public showpiece. In rather unclear language the treatise describes making a new opening in the nave wall (i.e. the blank upper nave wall typical

---

[22] The clack-valve, in this instance a loose metal flap blown open when air is sent from the bellows and falling back when air is sucked into them again.

of eleventh-century German churches?), with the organist in a room or passage behind. There is no mention of a wooden façade to the organ or even a simple exterior framework of the kind that can be found in Italian organs well into the nineteenth century. However, in discussing its location Theophilus is surely hinting at a larger organ than the single octave of three or four ranks: it cannot be for the sake of eight small front pipes that an arch in the wall has to be opened up?

Finally, the treatise gives the best-known description of a detail evidently found in some early organs and glimpsed now and then in the written sources: 'on the outside let there hang over the organ a thick cloth' shaped like a canopy, suspended from a pulley, and dropped down over the organ to keep it from dust. By mentioning the canopy's little wooden ball to which the rope is fastened Theophilus implies that he knew of such a structure, guaranteed, one would think, to bring dust with it.

Because of where the organ and bell chapters appear in the one copy of Theophilus's treatise that has them complete, it looks as if they were optional requirements – although in that case it is surprising that bells come after organs, for they were surely much more common. The organ described by Theophilus was probably not recent: 'theological positions' taken in his prologues are now recognized as typical of the period 1060–90, and his organ-technology (based on an actual organ examined by him?) could well belong to the same years. In such a treatise theoretical matters will be left open: calculations for pipe-measurements will not be included, since they belong to the sphere of theory, to the library rather than the workshop. But certain practical matters will equally be left open: there is no account of the organ's key-action (if it had any), of how many keys and rows of pipes there could be (if there were to be more than seven and three respectively), or how the chest-timber was actually hollowed out, all of which belonged to workshop practice.

A very early fifteen-note chest from a church in Grado (near Venice), as described and drawn in the sixteenth century,[23] shows sliders shaped at the player's end with elegant

---

[23] Zarlino: 290–1, reproduced in e.g. Perrot 1971: plate XXII.

little curves and circles, and two rows of pipe-holes. A pair of bellows was socketed into the back of the chest, which was one *braccio* ('forearm') long, one quarter wide, apparently of wood. This was clearly a small organ, but the only one putatively from the Theophilus period to leave any record. In its size and provision for detachable bellows, the organ would have been useful in processions of the traditional Mediterranean type.

Since master-craftsmen might have been able to read even if they could not write, Theophilus's three achievements (to observe objects, to order information and to write clear prose) could have given them one kind of organ, a first model on which to build or design their own instruments. On the basis of a master-craftsman's supervision, a workshop could make an organ with a compass of fifteen/sixteen or twenty-two/twenty-four notes, multiply rows of unison and octave pipes, and extrapolate the dimensions of bellows, trunk and chest accordingly. A woodworker could contrive a keyboard of sorts. But since there was probably not yet much in the way of joined timberwork in the church (no wooden stalls or screens), there was still no move to encase organs with wooden panels.

Organ-builders would also soon learn that if larger pipes were wanted, they would do well to follow techniques originally taught by the Romans for making cylindrical pipes of lead or pewter. A lead organ-pipe is not so totally different from a lead water-pipe except that its tendency to sag will be aggravated by being stood upright. Hardened alloys would soon have to be perfected. But how builders came to discard keys in the form of sliders (which were either noisy or tight) and devised press-keys operating a spring-loaded valve (a 'pallet', which was neither), is completely undocumented and needs to be looked at further. It is the structural detail on which the future of organs and organ-music depended.

Woodworking, Casework, Key-Action and Bellows

For many centuries specifics of woodworking are simply not described anywhere, and even 'workmen' in general are learned about only obliquely. But just as there is little documentation about craftsmen, so one cannot assume that they were dependent on written treatises or documentation produced by *their* predecessors: makers did not need to know any theory of levers from Archimedes or Hero or anyone else[24] to be able to conceive and make pivoted organ-keys. Nor did they have to wait for Greek descriptions of automaton mechanisms to circulate before they could devise means for transmitting the key's vertical movement across a horizontal distance.

Who 'they' were is likewise seldom recorded in documentation, and then incompletely. A certain gifted craftsman mentioned by the Venerable Bede in *c.*730 probably could not read, and he was almost certainly a lay worker, probably freelance, possibly itinerant (PL 95.254). However, to assume that craftsmen in the early medieval churches were predominantly laymen (Swartwout: 3ff) is to simplify the several categories or degrees of 'monk' and 'lay brother', as well as to ignore the difference between heavy and light crafts. The workmen whose places of work were drawn in the ninth-century *Plan of St Gall* (see p. 94) were part of the monastery's community, whether lay, novices or in deacon's orders, full monks on a rota or paid employees (*famuli*, 'servants').

Presumably certain monasteries specialized in machine-crafts as others did in handwriting or manuscript illumination, but being proficient in the background technologies would not lead to an organ unless there was some stimulus from those with particular interests in music or the liturgy. Twelfth-century Cistercian houses could and did develop all of the crafts, but organs were not wanted and were not developed by them. At the same time, given that there was the right kind of stimulus in a major monastery of the tenth century, one still has too little to go on to know who could make organs and what kind of instrument they would be. Casting copper alloy sheets from which to make pipes was no problem for major houses from Winchester to Hildesheim, or from the Meuse to the Po and the Ebro. But is it so that woodworking was still 'really based upon a Neolithic tradition' (Singer: 237), and techniques of hollowing-out, drilling

---

[24] Early understanding of levers must have been constantly accompanied by practical application of the principles behind them, little though such application got described in treatises.

and dowelling, such as the Romans already knew, were not yet able to produce an airtight box?

If so, one could imagine it being some time before wood would be used either as a major structural principle in organs or for elegant organ-façades. But the Anglo-Saxons already knew efficient joints in roof-beams, including lapjoints with dovetails, and their organs no doubt benefited from whatever woodworking skills were used for such special objects as Æthelwold's wheel at Abingdon or the bell-hangings at Winchester. But it was the early thirteenth century before screenwork was being regularly and conventionally built up from large, repeated sections of the kind that could have given the model for wood-encased organs. The backs of the stalls at Salisbury and Winchester (c.1245, c.1310) were a kind of ecclesiastical version of the wooden screen by then customarily dividing up the great halls of secular castles, as in the Tower of London (1237).[25]

Through accident of documentation, thirteenth-century English cathedrals and abbeys appear to have been particularly active in having major choirstalls built, leaving records of timber-purchases (St Paul's 1220, Peterborough 1233–45, Gloucester before 1237), in some cases other kinds of documentation concerning woodwork (Westminster c.1255), and here and there some extant remains (Rochester c.1227, Salisbury c.1245). These examples are all earlier than the complete extant set of stalls at Winchester, made at a time when, early in the next century, many other sets were beginning to appear.[26] Although stall-canopies or other superstructures may have been familiar in England before they were anywhere else, one can assume that the mid-thirteenth century saw a huge increase in the amount of timberwork in cathedral and monastic churches right across Europe.

One can also assume that with this activity went the building (and no doubt rebuilding) of more and more organs with wooden casework. In fact, although Theophilus specifies wood only for the chest and the trunking, it is difficult to

---

[25] Tower of London: 'spur of boards, good and becoming', according to Salzman: 260.
[26] For references and illustrations, see Tracy.

believe that craftsmen made no attempt to construct handsome protective casework for organs even before timber stalls became common. They must certainly have been attempting to provide an efficient key-mechanism and a firm bellows-structure, both of which depend on fine woodworking. In the absence of clear references, however, all this has to remain conjecture, and what a tenth-century or twelfth-century organ was like or how far its design was standardized may never be known. Assuming that by the later thirteenth century organs, like stalls, were probably being encased in panels and even integrated into the screen, such a new structure may well have been what was sometimes meant by the term *organa nova* in documents of the period (see p. 70).

When it comes to guessing how organs began to have suspended key-action, one is on very unsure ground. This action uses a spring not to return the key or slider to rest, but to keep closed an airtight valve (the pallet) located against the mouth of the wind-channel to the pipe, until pulled open by the wire from a lever (the key) which is 'suspended' from it. In its perfected form, it is a very sensitive, sophisticated mechanical system for organs, superseded only in the mid-nineteenth century, and then no more than as a temporary aberration. Probably the earliest form of this key-action was one in which the key did not pull the pallet open but pushed it down – i.e. when the row of pallets was not above the keys (as would become necessary when organs grew in size) but below, as in the small portable organs variously documented in the thirteenth century.

Pulling open a valve under the pipes may not seem to represent a giant technological step beyond pushing it open, but since it also enabled the pipes to be placed some way from the key that plays them, as is described below, a fair guess is that it was a later development originally explored for this very reason. Whatever the case, the 'suspended keyboard' that resulted and became the unrivalled mechanism for larger organs would have many advantages over the old slider keyboards – keys could be slim (finger-width), close-packed (only a working gap between) and easy to press (depending on the spring and the leverage). Hence the modern keyboard.

However, seeing such characteristics as *advantages* is

begging the question of what the keys played. If long-held notes were more useful for the clamour of festal music or for playing a siren-like triad out of doors, then there was no particular reason to aim at agility by rethinking traditional mechanisms. If the Aquincum organ did already aim at agility, it would be because it was a tiny organ for playing soprano melodies in intimate listening-spaces. In later centuries too, making slim finger-sized keys and packing them close together could come from making small-scale portable organs, not from any desire for finger-dexterity as such. However, once players became accustomed to playing nimbly on small organs, the more pressing became the need to find some way of making an agile mechanism for larger church organs. Above all, it would be important to have both the keys and the space between them not too large.

It was equally useful for large and small organs to find a means of distributing evenly the weight of the pipes on the chest, and it is possible that both of the two systems convenient for this originated in portable organs. In one, the wind was sent along a channel hollowed out in the top boards of the chest, from a key on the left side to a large and heavy pipe on the right. In the other, a wire from the key turned a rotating rod or roller (to one end of which it was attached), and this at its other end then pulled down a pallet. In both systems – channels or rollers – the pallet could be at some distance from the key, which meant that no key need have its own pipes directly above. Immediately, this would make it possible not only to distribute pipe-weight evenly but also to design many inventive organ-façades, with the pipes in many different sequences.

A third arrangement is also possible, although it does not help the weight problem because the pipes remain in sequence: the wires from the keys to the pallets were splayed outwards left and right, so that the chest could be longer than the keyboard. The bass pipes would then be some way to the left of the keyboard, the treble some way to the right, necessary if the compass were beyond a dozen or so notes. Splaying was a good system when the compass was not so very much longer than this, i.e. when the splay was not too pronounced. Quite possibly it also encouraged organ-builders to experiment with making, say, two short manuals rather than one long one. In no given organ before 1450 or so – such as the famous fourteenth-century instrument at Halberstadt, with its giant pipes – is it certain which of these systems was applied by its builder.

So far, no detail in any kind of source has been recognized as evidence for showing when pallets became known in organ-chests.[27] But by a rather telling coincidence, the later thirteenth century has recorded a comparable mechanical device built on a spring mechanism, if cruder and requiring less precision-work: the pole-lathe, where a spring-loaded rope is pulled down by the operator and on being released is pulled back up by its spring.[28] There is something of a parallel here to suspended key-action on an organ. Something else referred to in Theophilus's treatise would have helped the development of this mechanism: not in the organ chapters, but elsewhere, he describes a wire-drawing plate – the first author known to do so – which would produce a brass or iron wire suitable for pulling organ-pallets open. The pallet-spring itself could also be made from bent or coiled hardened wire, but for centuries the flat or leaf spring probably served well enough.[29]

As to bellows: the steps by which the whole skin became replaced by boards with flexible wedge-shaped leather panels – for both of which types Theophilus is a witness, though indistinctly for the second – are not known. Thir-teenth-century representations show various kinds of rounded, cylindrical or cuneiform bellows. Unlike chests or key-action, bellows did not obviously need to develop in any particular direction, since for more wind, one simply increased the number of small bellows. It is possible, there-fore, that really large cuneiform forge-bellows did not appear much earlier than the fourteenth century, by which

[27] Clack-valves, which pallets resemble in principle, are used for both inflow and outflow of extant Roman bronze pumps in Madrid (Museo Arqueológico Nacional) and London (British Museum).

[28] This is a lathe-structure in which a flexible pole above the operator's head holds one end of a rope which is fastened at the other to a foot-lever and in between wound around the axle of a lathe. The foot pulls the rope down, it turns the axle, and the beam pulls it up again.

[29] The oldest extant organ pallet-springs, in the organ of Norrlanda (claimed to be late fourteenth century – see Kjersgaard), are U-shaped leaf springs.

time mechanical means were being devised to raise them by large turning wheels, in industry (water-powered wheels) and in churches (hand-powered wheels?).[30]

One would also expect by now that organ-builders understood the principle of the wind-reservoir, as Theophilus did with his wind-collector. With such a system, the wind and the sound it produces are stabilized by the wind being sent from the bellows not direct to the chest, but first into a reservoir, like the bag of a bagpipes or the cistern of a water-organ. For sustained music of all kinds, any such device was advisable.

Hints of the Organ to Come?

Equally open to educated guesswork are how many notes there were to the octave in an organ after Theophilus's period and how early the sharps were known. If a thirteenth-century theorist of northern France refers to only two sharps in the scale (F-sharp and G-sharp in the *Summa musice* – GS 3.221), one can be sure that builders he did not know about were making more, and that here and there, particularly on smaller organs, C-sharp and D-sharp were becoming known. But none of them is likely on a keyboard that did not already have B-flat.

The sharps would be especially useful for three things: ornate melodies in the treble, harmonies in three parts or voices, and transposition from one pitch to another. While on most keyboards into the fourteenth century B-flat probably remained a 'natural' key (not a raised 'accidental', or only a little higher than naturals), equally probable is that all the sharps were normally raised, particularly on portable instruments in which all dimensions needed to be as compact as possible. Obviously, on small organs the keyboard, the action and the pipes were not only modest in size but were also all designed for playing decorative treble melodies. Not before the fifteenth century and its various newly invented instruments would keyboards themselves become more or less

---

[30] French examples from the fourteenth century are: water power for the bellows of a forge (in Gille: 15); and a wheel, presumably tripping the organ-bellows and turned by six or seven servants, at Notre-Dame, Paris (in Wright: 146).

standardized over the whole range of musical instruments that had them.

As to the pipes: since so little is known about the way organs earlier than the fourteenth century actually worked, the more than two hundred pipes thought to date from before 1200 and found in Bethlehem in 1906 may, when fully described and understood, yield good information about the period after Theophilus. They are assumed to be European, not Arabic; most are open cylindrical copper-alloy pipes, and their lengths (c.16–105 cm) allow some three octaves of sound (see Montagu). While they say nothing about how the organ worked, they do raise again one of the most crucial questions in the history of organs, that concerning the material of pipes.

For both types of pipe-metal – copper alloys and lead alloys – the Romans had bequeathed particular technologies to their empire and had had different uses for each. Tin was common to both. Probably pipes of copper or bronze had always been preferred for the sake of durability and looks rather than for tone, and in less than luxurious circumstances (particularly in England?), the copper element in bronze was no doubt low unless special funding were available, as it evidently was at Ramsey in the late tenth century. A form of copper-hardened tin must have been known, and perhaps some areas such as Frisia and Saxonia developed base alloys from an early period, using tin in small percentages. The importance of all this is that the more easily worked pewters would have allowed makers to roll bigger pipes, and therefore to enlarge tonal range beyond the old Mediterranean water-organ with its copper alloy pipes.

Anglo-Saxon objects of pewter in the British Museum suggest that making pipes with a high or low tin content would have presented no great difficulty to craftsmen, and perhaps such things were particularly developed in England. By the twelfth century tin's several uses were being described by Theophilus, though not, significantly, for organ pipes; was he simply out of date? Only a century and a half later, highly polished tin was being specified in various Italian contracts (Donati: 149–50) and played a big part in organ-façades as casework was being developed in the later thirteenth century. Pipes looked like cylinders of bright silver and thus corresponded to the gilt bronzes of an earlier period.

Increasing use of pewter by organ-builders leads to two intriguing questions about music history. One of them is technical: Did tin, being practicable for rolling and soldering on a larger scale than copper, prompt a greater compass for keyboards or merely make it possible? One could argue either way, but the first (which implies that instrument-making encouraged musical developments rather than vice versa) seems to me more likely than the second. The other question follows on from this and is even more speculative: If the large pipes of the fourteenth century were made – as they surely were – of a tin alloy, must the evolution of the bass line in music (see chapter 1) be credited in part to organ-builders moving from copper pipes to pewter? I think the answer must be yes.

Although the two other regular kinds of organ-pipe – reeds and wooden pipes – seem to belong to the fifteenth-century cult of small-scale and secular keyboard instruments, there are earlier hints of them. It is unlikely that the Aquincum builder would use stoppers purely for fine-tuning and not for the sake of the tone and the pitch they produce. Similarly, reed-tongues must have at least sometimes supplied the sound for the trumpets blown by Hero's automatic statues in Hellenistic times. And the four large extant wooden pipes substituting for metal bass pipes in S. Petronio, Bologna (1471–5), were surely not the first of their kind. But none of these types is likely to have appeared regularly before 1400 or even later, and for centuries the standard organ-chorus doubtless consisted only of open metal pipes of unisons and octaves grouped for each key.

The development of this chorus is a big question. However or wherever fifth-sounding ranks ('quints') developed, they were less common or obvious to the ear than they became in later organs and are usually assumed to have been in earlier. In 1475, the organ of S. Petronio, Bologna was still producing relatively few quints for the note Middle C:

three unison pipes (8.8.8)
two octave pipes below (16.16)
two octave pipes above, and three superoctaves (4.4 plus 2.1.1)
three single quints (2⅔.1⅓.⅔)

No doubt theory lagged behind practice in the question of how to reinforce tone in a large building. In general, however, there is so little evidence that fifth-sounding ranks were prominent that a question often asked by music historians – Was vocal organum so called because voices singing parallel fifths imitated the fifth-sounding pipes in an organ chorus? – now appears to arise not only from a misunderstanding of the term *organum* for vocal counterpoint but from a misunderstanding of organs themselves. In addition, even when present, the 'fifth-sounding' pipes of organs will have sounded not at the fifth but at the twelfth or nineteenth, except for the topmost notes.

Again, there is little evidence on which to base conjectures about the way the familiar sound of 'Full Organ' came about. One particular early theorist (south German, eleventh century)[31] alludes to a chorus containing 'as many pipes as musicians are used to placing in the organ' *(tot fistulis . . . musici solent . . . organico instrumento apponere)*, but goes on to specify only suboctaves, 'for the sake of sweetness and elegance' *(suavitatis et ornatus causa* – Sachs 1970: 126). This could mean either that the organ went down a further octave or that each note on an organ had its lower octave, even both. The difference between those two need not concern a theorist, and the very ambiguity may mean that builders were working with various octave pitches, the more of them the bigger the organ. It would be the big pipes that aroused the interest of musicians, being newer, rarer and technically more admirable.

But the treble part of the compass would also have made demands on the builder. Working in the big gothic churches of the period, as they increasingly were, organ-builders must often have been struck by the need to boost the high notes. Since Roman times, the part of the organ-compass known to instrument-makers had been the upper part, and multiple rows of pipes would always have been necessary when a penetrating sound was required, for carrying power in processions or in arenas. It is hard to believe that the organs once used for noise in the public events of both Old and New Rome had no fifth-sounding pipes at all in their little treble

---

[31] Assumed by Gerbert (GS 2) to be Eberhard of Freising, perhaps a pupil of William of Hirsau; further discussion in Sachs 1980: 213–14.

compasses, even if they were not prominent enough in the total sound to give the impression that one was hearing 'parallel fifths'.

By the late fourteenth century, according to the theorist Arnulf of St-Ghislain, there were clergy *(clericos)*

qui in organicis instrumentis	who on *organic instruments*
difficilimos musicales modulos	devise and teach [?] the
quos exprimere vix	most difficult passages of music,
praesumeret vox humana	which the human voice would
adinveniunt atque tradunt.	hardly presume to perform.
(GS 3.316)	

Three interesting details in Arnulf's remark are that the voice and what it can do are a touchstone, that 'music' means much as it does today, and that 'difficulty' is coming in as a quality in musical performance. Assuming that *organicis instrumentis* can include the organ, and that the words are more than merely a new complaint about gifted clergy-musicians playing brilliant secular music, keyboard-making itself would clearly have had to make it possible to play in such a virtuoso manner. This would imply as much about organ-technology as about music, and both must by now have reached a stage unforeseen by those churches in the West that had been the first to have them. The whole reference seems typical of the High Middle Ages and far from the world of monastic reformers in the year 1000.

References

Acta SS = J. Bollandus, *Acta sanctorum quotquot toto orbe coluntur* (Amsterdam et al., 1643–), ed. J. Carnandet (1863–).

Anglés = H. Anglés, *Scripta musicologica*, ed. T. López-Calo, 3 vols (Rome, 1975–6).

Aubry = P. Aubry, 'Les abus de la musique d'église au XIIe et au XIIIe siècle', *La Tribune de Saint-Gervais* 9 (1903), pp. 57–62.

Babb = W. Babb (trans.), *Hucbald, Guido and John on Music*, ed. C. V. Palisca (New Haven: Yale Univerity Press, 1978).

Baldelló = F. Baldelló, 'Organos y organeros en Barcelona (siglos XIII–XIX)', *Anuario musical* 1 (1946), pp. 195–237.

Becker = J. Becker (ed.), *Liudprandi episcopi cremonensis opera*, Scriptores rerum germanicarum i.u.s (Hanover/Leipzig: Hahn, 1915).

Bird = W. H. B. Bird (ed.), *Calendar of the MSS of the Dean and Chapter of Wells* (London: Historical MSS Commission, 1907).

Bischoff = B. Bischoff, 'Eine Beschreibung der Basilika von Saint-Denis aus dem Jahre 799', *Kunstchronik* 34 (1981), pp. 97–103.

Bösken = F. Bösken, 'Beiträge zur Orgelgeschichte des Mittelrheins bis zum Beginn des 16. Jahrhunderts', *Kirchenmusikalisches Jahrbuch* 45 (1961), pp. 82–101.

Buhle = E. Buhle, *Die musikalischen Instrumente in den Miniaturen des frühen Mittelalters. Ein Beitrag zur Geschichte der Musikinstrumente, 1: Die Blasinstrumente* (Leipzig, 1903).

Callebat = L. Callebat, *Vitruve de l'Architecture Livre X* (Paris, 1986).

Campbell = Alistair Campbell, *Frithegodi monachi breuiloquium vitae beati Wilfredi et Wulfstani cantoris narratio metrica de Sancto Swithuno* (Zürich: Thesauri Mundi, 1950), p. 69f.

Connolly = T. H. Connolly, 'The Legend of St Cecilia: 1, The Origins of the Cult', *Studi musicali* 7 (1978), pp. 3–37.

CSM = *Corpus scriptorum de musica*.

Davis-Weyer = C. Davis-Weyer, *Early Medieval Art 300–1150: Sources and Documents*, Mediaeval Academy Reprints for Teaching 17 (1971; Toronto: University of Toronto Press, 1986).

Dodwell = C. R. Dodwell, *Theophilus, De diuersis artibus. The Various*

Arts, Translated from the Latin with Introduction and Notes (London, 1961).

Donati = P. P. Donati, 'Regesto documentario', in P. P. Donati et al. (ed.), *Arte nell'Aretino seconda mostra di restauri dal 1975 al 1979 . . . Catalogo* (Florence, [1979]), pp. 148–261.

Dreves = G. M. Dreves (ed.), *Analecta hymnica medii aevi*, 55 vols (Leipzig: Reisland, 1886–1922).

Du Cange = Charles Du Cange, *Glossarium ad scriptores mediae et infimae latinitatis* (Paris, 1678).

Erskine = A. M. Erskine, *The Accounts of the Fabric of Exeter Cathedral, 1279–1353* (Torquay, 1981).

Farmer = Henry George Farmer, *The Organ of the Ancients from Eastern Sources (Hebrew, Syriac and Arabic)* (London: Reeves, 1931).

FRB = N. Palacky (ed.) [1–3] and J. Emler (ed.) [4–5], *Fontes rerum bohemicarum*, 5 vols (Prague, 1873–93).

Freeman = A. Freeman, 'The Organs of York Minster', *The Organ* 5 (1926), pp. 193–204.

Gille = B. Gille, *Les origines de la grande industrie métallurgique en France* (Paris, 1947).

Goodman = A. W. Goodman, *Chartulary of Winchester Cathedral* (London, 1927).

GS = M. Gerbert (ed.), *Scriptores ecclesiastici de musica sacra potissimum*, 3 vols (St Blasien, 1784).

Hammerstein = R. Hammerstein, *Macht und Klang. Tönende Automaten als Realitäten und Fiktion in der alten und mittelalterlichen Welt* (Bern, 1986).

Holschneider 1968 = Andreas Holschneider, *Die Organa von Winchester: Studien zum ältesten Repertoire polyphoner Musik* (Hildesheim: Olms, 1968).

Holschneider 1978 = A. Holschneider, 'Die instrumentalen Tonbuchstaben im Winchester Troper', in T. Kohlhase and V. Scherliess (ed.), *Festschrift Georg von Dadelsen zum 60 Geburtstag* (Neuhausen-Stuttgart: Hänssler, 1978), pp. 155–66.

Horst = K. van der Horst and J. H. A. Engelbregt, *Utrecht Psalter = Codices selecti phototypice impressi, Facsimile* LXXV (Graz, 1982), *Kommentar* LXXV (Graz, 1984).

Johnson = C. Johnson, *Registrum Hamonis Hethe Diocesis Roffensis AD 1319–1352*, Canterbury & York Series 48 (Oxford, 1948).

Kaba = M. Kaba, *Die römische Orgel von Aquincum (3. Jahrhundert)*, Musicologia hungarica 6 (Budapest, 1976).

Kelly = T. F. Kelly, 'Early Polyphony at Montecassino', in F. Della Seta and F. Piperno (ed.), *In cantu et in sermone: For Nino Pirrotta on his 80th Birthday* (Florence: Olschki, 1989), pp. 1–5.

Kjersgaard = M. Kjersgaard, 'Technical Aspects of Swedish Organ-Building during the Middle Ages', *ISO Information* 27 (1987), pp.

5–118, and 29 (1988), pp 29–30.

Lapidge & Rosier = M. Lapidge and James L. Rosier, *Aldhelm: The Poetic Works* (Cambridge, 1985).

Llovera = J.-M. Garcia Llovera, *De organo vetere hispanico: zur Frühgeschichte der Orgel in Spanien* (St Ottilien, 1987).

Marca = Petrus de Marca, *Marca hispanica sive limes hispanicus* (Paris, 1688).

Matthier = Andrea L. Matthier, 'The Medieval Wheelbarrow', *Technology & Culture* 32 (1991), pp. 356–64.

Mellows = W. T. Mellows (ed.), *The Chronicle of Hugh Candidus, a Monk of Peterborough* (Oxford: OUP, 1949).

MGH AA = *Monumenta Germaniae Historica, Auctores antiquissimi*, 15 vols (1877–1919).

MGH Cap = *MGH Capitularia regum francorum* = *Legum Sectio ii*, 2 vols (1883–97).

MGH Epist = *MGH Epistolae merowingici et carolini aevi*, 5 vols (1892–1939).

MGH Poet lat = *MGH Poetae latinae aevi carolini*, 4 vols (1881–99).

MGH SS = *MGH Scriptores in folio*, 34 vols (1824–1980).

Montagu = J. Montagu, 'The Oldest Organ in Christendom', *Fellowship of Makers and Researchers of Historical Instruments Quarterly* 35 (April, 1984), pp. 51–2.

Morgan = M. H. Morgan, *Vitruvius: The Ten Books of Architecture* (New York, 1914).

NOHM = Richard Crocker and David Hiley (ed.), *The New Oxford History of Music*, vol. 2: *The Early Middle Ages to 1300* (Oxford: OUP, 1990).

Parsons = David Parsons, 'Sites and Monuments of the Anglo-Saxon Mission in Central Germany', *The Archaeological Journal* 140 (1983), pp. 280–321.

Perrot 1965 = Jean Perrot, *L'Orgue de ses origines hellénistiques à la fin du XIIIe siècle: Étude historique et archéologique* (Paris: Picard, 1965).

Perrot 1971 = Jean Perrot, *The Organ from its Invention in the Hellenistic Period to the End of the Thirteenth Century*, trans. Norma Deane (London, 1971).

PL = J. P. Migne (ed.), *Patrologiae cursus completus, series latina*, 221 vols (Paris, 1844–64).

Price = Percival Price, *Bells and Man* (Oxford: OUP, 1983).

Raine = J. Raine (ed.), *Historiae Dunelmensis Scriptores Tres*, Publications of the Surtees Society 9 (London/Edinburgh, 1839).

RBMAS = *Rerum britannicarum medii aevi scriptores* [= Rolls Series].

Sachs 1970 = Klaus-Jürgen Sachs, *Mensura fistularum: die Mensurierung der Orgelpfeifen im Mittelalter 1, Edition der Texte*, Schriftenreihe der Walcker-Stiftung für orgelwissenschaftliche Forschung 1 (Stuttgart: Musikwiss. Verlags-Ges., 1970).

Sachs 1972 = K.-J. Sachs, 'Gerbertus cognomento musicus. Zur musikgeschichtlichen Stellung des Gerbert von Reims (nachmaligen Papstes Sylvester II.)', *Archiv für Musikwissenschaft* 29 (1972), pp. 257–74.

Sachs 1980 = K.-J. Sachs, *Mensura fistularum. Die Mensurierung der Orgelpfeifen im Mittelalter, II Studien zur Tradition und Kommentar der Texte* (Murrhardt: Musikwiss. Verlags-Ges., 1980).

Salzman = L. F. Salzman, *Building in England down to 1540: A Documentary History* (Oxford, 1952).

Sanderson = W. Sanderson, 'The Plan of St Gall Reconsidered', *Speculum* 60 (1985), pp. 615–32.

Schmidt = W. Schmidt, *Herons von Alexandria Druckwerke und Automatentheater: 1 Pneumatica et Automata* (Leipzig, 1899).

Schuberth = D. Schuberth, *Kaiserliche Liturgie. Die Einbeziehung von Musikinstrumente, insbesondere der Orgel, in den frühchristlichen Gottesdienst,* Veröffentlichungen der evangelischen Gesellschaft für Liturgieforschung 17 (Göttingen: Vandenhoeck, 1968).

Seebass = T. Seebass, *Musikdarstellung und Psalterillustration im früheren Mittelalter* (Bern: Francke, 1973).

Senhal = J. Senhal, 'Die Orgeln der Olmützer Kathedrale', *Acta organologica* 15 (1981), pp. 27–75.

Singer = C. Singer et al. (ed.), *A History of Technology*, vol 2: *The Mediterranean Civilizations and the Middle Ages c.700BC–c.1500AD* (Oxford, 1957).

Stubbs = C. W. Stubbs, *Historical Memorials of Ely Cathedral* (London, 1897).

Stuttgart = *Der Stuttgarter Bilderpsalter* [Facsimile and Commentary], 2 vols (Stuttgart, 1968).

Sullivan = R. E. Sullivan, 'The Carolingian Missionary and the Pagan', *Speculum* 28 (1953), pp. 705–40.

Swartwout = R. E. Swartwout, *The Monastic Craftsman* (Cambridge, 1932).

Taucci = R. Taucci, *Rivista di studi storici sull'Ordine dei Servi di Maria,* vol 2: *Fra Andrea dei Servi organista e compositore del Trecento* (Rome, 1935), pp. 73–108.

Thompson = E. M. Thompson (ed.), *The Customary of the Benedictine Monasteries of St Augustine, Canterbury and St Peter, Westminster,* Henry Bradshaw Society 23 and 28 (London, 1902, 1904).

Tracy = C. Tracy, *English Gothic Choir-Stalls 1200–1400* (Woodbridge, 1987).

Usher = A. P. Usher, *A History of Mechanical Inventions* (New York, 1929).

Walcker-Mayer = W. Walcker-Mayer, *The Roman Organ of Aquincum,* trans. J. Godwin (Ludwigsburg, 1972).

Wallace-Hadrill 1960 = J. M. Wallace-Hadrill, *Fredegarii*

chronicorum liber quartus cum continuationibus (London: OUP, 1960).

Wallace-Hadrill 1983 = J. M. Wallace-Hadrill, *The Frankish Church* (Oxford: Clarendon, 1983).

Willis = R. Willis, *The Architectural History of Canterbury Cathedral* (London, 1845).

Wright = C. Wright, *Music and Ceremony at Notre Dame of Paris 500–1500* (Cambridge: CUP, 1989).

Zarlino = G. Zarlino, *Sopplimenti musicali* (Venice, 1588).

Zettler = A. Zettler, *Die frühen Klosterbauten der Reichenau: Ausgrabungen – Schriftquellen – St. Galler Klosterplan,* Freiburger Forschungen zum ersten Jahrtausend in Südwestdeutschland 3 (Sigmaringen, 1988).

Zolnay = L. Zolnay, 'Ungarische Orgelbauer und Organisten im 14.–16. Jahrhundert', *Studia musicologica* 14 (1972), pp. 385–400.

Index

INDEX

St Albans 81, 97
St Blasien 67
St-Denis 4, 6, 73, 75
St Gall 36, 50–2, 67, 80, 89–90, 107–8
St-Germain-des-Prés 110
St-Riquier 90, 93, 95
St-Wandrille 65
Strasbourg 70
Stubbs, C. W. 69n
Stuttgart Psalter 25, 108–111
Suavians, the 3
Sullivan, R. E. 49n, 50
Swartwout, R. E. 127
Swithun, Saint 114n

Tacitus 49
Tallis, T. 120
Tarragona 71
Taucci, R. 72
Tavara 52n
Te deum 80–2, 86, 97, 119
Tertullian 25
Theodoric II, King 21
Theodosius, Emperor 20, 29
Theophilos, Emperor 30
Theophilus, monk 16, 20, 31, 62–3, 96, 100, 104, 110, 121–6, 128, 131–3
Thomas Becket, Saint 69
Thompson, E. M. 98n
Tolomeo of Lucca 45
Toul 90
Tours 49–50
Tracy, C. 128
Treviso 72n
tropes 78–80, 82
Tuotilo of St Gall 79

Ungar, J. 120

Usher, A. P. 113–14
Utrecht Psalter 31, 39, 108–11, 120

Van der Goes, and Van Eyck 112
Verdun 90
Vich 57
Vikings, the 51, 69, 94–5
Virdung, Sebastian 43
Virgil 119
Vitalian, Pope 44–6, 56
Vitruvius 16–20, 31, 33, 39, 104, 113–14, 122

Walahfrid Strabo 38–9
Walcker-Mayer, W. 113
Wallace-Hadrill, J. M. 35n, 48n
Water Newton 27n
Wells 72
Werden 92
Westminster 128
William of Hirsau 89, 106, 135n
William of Malmesbury 50n, 51, 59–61
Willibald, Saint 47
Willis, R. 68n
Winchester 3, 13, 20, 37, 50 57–60, 69, 76, 78–80, 87–92, 96, 109, 114–21, 127–8
Worcester 63
Worms 70
Wright, C. 98, 132n
Wulfstan, Cantor 28, 50n, 57–8, 78, 91–2, 96, 100, 109, 114–21

York 66, 72

Zarlino, G. 125n
Zettler, A. 93n
Zliten 21
Zolnay, L. 71n